SUNDAY ADELAJA

How To Become Great Through Time Conversion

Sunday Adelaja

HOW TO BECOME GREAT THROUGH TIME CONVERSION

©2017 Sunday Adelaja

ISBN 978-1-908040-82-4

Cover design by Oleksander Bondaruk

Interior design by Oleksander Bondaruk

CONTENTS

INTRODUCTION

Dear friends, the world is sitting on a gold mine but knows it not. The world has been given a treasure through which its inhabitants can attain greatness if they so desire. This treasure is available to and equally distributed to all men. It is however shocking to find that despite the fact that all men have this treasure that could make them great, we don't see all men living in greatness in reality. The question then is how come only a few are great in the real sense of the word. What about others! Why do we have only a few superstars? Why are all other people not great? Well, the reason is because only a few have discovered that through this treasure all men could become great. What is this treasure of which I speak? The treasure I am talking about is the treasure of TIME. Yes! Time. The reason why one man is great and another is not is simply because one man discovered the power of time while the other did not. The difference between people is in how well they understand the treasure of time and what they did with their time.

In this book I am revealing to you that you can become great just by simply understanding what to do with your time. You can leave your mark in the sand of history just by discovering the secrets of greatness through time conversion. I want you to leave your mark in the sand of history. There is no one who was supposed to come to this world and leave empty. You are not supposed to be here in this world and not leave something for which you could be called great. **Greatness is an attainment that is bought with the currency of time.**

I want to challenge you through this book that you were endowed with this treasure of time so that you could buy greatness with it. You can become whatever you want to become just by applying the principles of time conversion that are in this book.

However this gift of time will not always be yours forever. It diminishes as the day passes. Time melts away in every passing moment. The shocking thing about this passing time is that as time diminishes your life also diminishes with it. The secret of all greatness is to not allow time diminish without converting it into a product of greatness. What I therefore seek to achieve through this book is to teach you how you could convert your diminishing life into some products of greatness. I want to sow so much seed in you that you will become pregnant with the seed of greatness. My intention is to teach you how to stop wasting your time because to waste time is to waste life. My primary aim is to show you principles through which you could invest your time and buy greatness with it.

It is my utmost desire that by the time you finish reading this book, you will become pregnant with visions, and you will become pregnant with projects. You will become so great that the world will wonder how it all happened.

Read on my friends and join the league of great names like Salvador Dali, Michelangelo, Johann Sebastian Bach, Beethoven, Thomas Edison, Sir Isaac Newton, etc. who through the power of time conversion left their mark in the sand of history.

Go ahead and climb this ladder of greatness! See you at the top!

CHAPTER 1

GREATNESS IS A PRODUCT OF TIME

EVERYONE CAN BECOME GREAT

We live in a world that has given us a wrong impression and lied to us about what it takes to be great. Our world has deceived us into thinking that only a few selected people could be great. We have been made to believe a lie that we don't all have equal potentials to become great. You see! I disagree with that. You know what! Everybody, including you, potentially can be great. It is not only some few people who could be great.

The majority of people on earth think that God specially chooses those who he wants to become great. But how can that be true? If God created all men, then it will be unfair for him to select only a few from the lot to make them great. That will be favoritism but we all know that God doesn't show favoritism neither does he discriminate. If God were to select those who will be great, what criteria would he use? Dear friends, let me tell you the truth. When it comes to greatness, God doesn't choose for man. He has created all men equally to become great.

Looking at the world today, you can attest to the fact that you don't see that everyone is great. You could see only a few great men and superstars. What has happened to the rest of the world? Why are they not great also? Well, the answer to that question is simple and not far-fetched. Those who have become great have only discovered something that the rest of the world has not discovered. Those who are great know a secret that the remaining lot do not know. The only thing that is limiting me and you from attaining anything in life is what we know or what we don't know. The question, therefore, is "what is the secret of the great? What do they know that you and the rest of the world are ignorant of?" Just read on a little further. I am going to be revealing that secret to you shortly.

Meanwhile, just know that I want you to leave your mark in the sand of history. There is no one who was supposed to come to this world and leave empty. You are not supposed to be here in this world and not leave something for which you could be called great. Every one of us has that potential to be great. You have the seed of greatness in you already. If you don't believe it, I am going to activate the consciousness in your mind through this book. The seed of greatness is in you but you have to know it in your mind. I am going to make the seed of greatness come alive in your awareness and into your consciousness until you begin to breathe and think greatness. This is so that you can start believing that there is nothing you cannot do. And it is true! You are capable of everything and of anything. By the time you finish reading and applying the principles that are in this book, you will not only be dreaming of conceiving or giving birth to one product, you will have so many projects and products that you are going to give birth to for which the world and your generation will remember you.

I want you to look at greatness, not as something that is meant or reserved for some special people somewhere. My aim is to try to make you start seeing greatness as something that is attainable to you. The secret I am trying to reveal to you is that greatness is under your power. Greatness is not greater than you. You have total control over greatness. You can decide to be great and it will happen. Not only can you decide to be great, you also have the power to determine the height of your greatness. The truth I am trying to bring to your awareness is that it is not your society nor your place of birth that determines your greatness. The key to your greatness is not in the hands of your parents neither is it in the hands of your country's president or governors. It is not even the government and economic status of your country that decides whether or not you will be great. The key to your greatness is under your control. You are the one in charge of your life and how great you become is up to you.

I know you may be thinking that greatness is not possible with you and that it is reserved for some special people. I, however, want to disagree with your ideology of greatness. I also want you to review the idea of greatness that the world has made you believe in. I want you to refuse the theory that states that only some certain people have the likelihood of becoming great. I want you to re-adjust your mindset and begin to believe with me that you too can become great. All I am saying is that you should begin to see greatness as something you cannot do without. Begin to see greatness as something that you cannot afford not to have. In fact, it is unpardonable for you to leave this world without recording some greatness in your account.

> *"You were born with potential. You*
> *were born with goodness and trust.*
> *You were born with ideals and dreams.*
> *You were born with greatness. You*
> *were born with wings. You are not*
> *meant for crawling, so don't. You have*
> *wings. Learn to use them and fly."*
> JALALUDDIN RUMI

You can leave your mark in the sand of history. You can do something remarkable with your life. You have what it takes to leave your footprint in the sand of history. It is easy. It is ordinary and it is possible. Life is predictable. You can predict the outcome of your life. You can chart your own way. You can break your own record. You can write your own history of greatness and I am going to show you how to do all that.

GREATNESS CAN BE BOUGHT

The truth I have been trying to reveal to you is that you can become great through the currency of time. Let me show you one secret that I have been trying to communicate to you from the beginning of this book. The secret is this: **Greatness is an attainment that is bought with the currency of time.** I want you to give this statement a thought and let it sink down into your subconscious. People who have become great have only become great because they bought that greatness. They purchased that greatness but only with the currency of time. The reason I said greatness can be bought is because anything anybody ever attained in life was achieved because it was purchased. Anything anybody has was purchased with the currency of time. In fact, the house you are living in was built and purchased by you by the currency of time. The car that you ride on was purchased by you with the currency of time. But you may want to say "but I bought my car with money not with time" Well! Let me explain it to you. Let's assume that your car cost twenty thousand US dollars. You invested a certain amount of time for you to make that amount of money. Let's imagine that you earn ten dollars an hour, which means you have to work so many days and for so many months before you could make twenty thousand US dollars. Therefore twenty thousand US dollars is the amount of time you dedicated to making that money. You gave out a part of your life in order to get that money. You gave out a fragment of your life, exchanging your life and your time for that amount of money. Let's say you work for eight hours every day. It will cost you about twelve and half months of working every working day to be able to earn up to that twenty thousand US dollar. What you did was to give out twelve and half months of your life in exchange for a car. If we also assume that you worked for ten years to be able to build a house, then what you did was to give out ten years of your life in exchange for a house. Therefore it was your time that you gave out to work that bought the car or the house. Hence, everything you have is bought by the currency of time.

You could say "but I didn't spend so much buying it, I just got a loan from the bank to buy it" You see, it's the same thing whether you worked to buy the house or you took a loan to buy it. Even though you are staying in the house now, you have already mortgaged or sold the next ten years of your life. You are still going to use the currency of time to pay for that house. It's still going to be the currency of time because even though the money was given to you by the bank, you are going to sell ten years of your future to be able to pay back your loan. That is why when banks give you a loan for a house, you sign a contract with them that you are going to be paying it back for the next ten years or twenty years as the case may be. This means you are actually mortgaging ten or twenty years of your future to be able to pay back. You have already given away the ten or twenty years that you have not lived yet, that is still to come in exchange for a house. What a tragedy! How could you convert your whole life just for a car or a house! How could you exchange a whole life just for a car or a house!

So the next time you want to buy a car or a house, don't be deceived into thinking that you are going to buy it with money. No! You are not buying it with money, you are buying it with your life. It is your life that is being mortgaged. Why will you spend your life just like that when you could invest it!

What I have been trying to prove to you is that everything that you have was bought by the currency of time. Greatness like every other product is bought with the currency of time. You can buy greatness by the currency of time. What I am saying is that greatness can only be bought through time. It is the time that delivers greatness to people. Therefore if you can know how to convert your time by investing it, then you can buy greatness with it. Your life is not meant to be used in exchange for mundane things like houses and cars but to purchase greatness.

I am about to tell you the story of a man who became great because he understood the importance of time management.

THE BENJAMIN FRANKLIN STORY

No one can mention the great names in history without mentioning the name Benjamin Franklin. He was a publisher and author, a scientist and inventor, a civic leader, and a diplomat.

Benjamin Franklin was born January 17, 1706. His family was polygamous and poor. His father married two wives and had 17 children. His father was a candle maker and Benjamin was introduced to the candle making business at an early age. He was also involved with his brother's printing shop. Benjamin was a voracious reader who invested any free time he had into reading books and learning about a wide range of subjects. Whilst co-workers would waste away their lunch break, Benjamin Franklin would meditate on books from the bookshop digesting as much information as he could get within that short time.

Benjamin loved prose writing and at an early age, he started writing articles which were published under a pseudonym. After several were published, he revealed to his father that he was the one who wrote them. At age 17, the young Benjamin left the family business and traveled to Philadelphia. In Philadelphia, Benjamin's reputation as a prolific writer increased. Later on, he took a job offer in England from Governor William Keith but he was later abandoned by the governor without salary. Benjamin soon became poor with no money. However, because of his natural resourcefulness and determination, he soon overcame those difficult times. Benjamin later found a printing job in London.

You may be wondering why Benjamin franklin was mentioned among the great names in history. Was he truly great? The answer is yes! Benjamin franklin was one of the great names that history has to offer. The question I seek to address in this book is "how did he become great?" To answer that question, I want us to review his early years as a child and agree on two things that were the stepping stones to his greatness. The first and most important of all is that Benjamin franklin invested his time into reading books. He understood that the best thing to do with time was to invest it into learning and adding value to one's life. While his colleagues at work would just while away their break time, Benjamin Franklin would rather invest that time into reading books. That was his foundation for greatness. He didn't allow his time to be wasted but made sure he converted the time into increasing his knowledge. We could conclude that Benjamin became great because he bought that greatness by investing his time wisely. One could attest to that fact by considering his view of time as stated in his words:

"You may delay, but time will not"
BENJAMIN FRANKLIN

*"Never leave till tomorrow which
you can do today"*
BENJAMIN FRANKLIN

From the quotes above, Benjamin Franklin was saying that you should not waste time by allowing it pass by without doing anything with it. He said time doesn't delay, which means that time keeps moving and passing by whether you delay or not. Time doesn't procrastinate its passing by, it moves always. Benjamin was also saying that since time doesn't delay, don't leave till tomorrow what you can do today. In other words, act now, invest time now into doing something valuable. Don't sit back and watch time just pass by unused. If he didn't invest time into studying and reading, he would not have become great. If he didn't invest time into writing and publishing his articles, he would not have become great. He became renown because he properly invested his time.

The second thing about his life was that though he was poor, he still became great. How could a poor man from a poor background become great? The answer is "greatness is not dependent on your background. It is dependent on how much value you were able to add to yourself per time. Though he was from a poor background, yet he constantly added value to himself by voraciously reading books and studying painstakingly. Most people have used their poor background as an excuse to live a life of mediocrity but not Benjamin Franklin. The determination, the time investment and self-taught success of his early years showed the world the real man behind the legend: a man who rose from poor beginnings to build fame, fortune, and influence through sheer will, a man who changed the quality of life for millions and helped free a nation from tyranny.

TIME MANAGEMENT FORMULAS FROM BENJAMIN FRANKLIN'S LIFE

Dear friends, if you truly desire to be great, you must understand time management. It is the secret of all great people in history. They knew what best to do with time. Benjamin franklin wrote down 12 habits or virtues he wanted to improve in his life. One of the habits talks about being industrious by proper time management. Considering his view on time management and his quotes on time, I want to explain a few facts that we could learn from Benjamin Franklin's life that is most relevant to the subject matter of this book. I will call them formulas for effective time management. You too can become great by applying these formulas to your everyday life.

FORMULA 1: Cut your goals into tiny units of work, and think only about one unit at a time.

Most people write down goals that they never achieve. The reason why most of your goals are probably not achieved is because you do not break down your goals into smaller units of work. To be effective in fulfilling your goals, you must break them down into little tasks and then spend most of your time working on the task in front of you, instead of being overwhelmed by the enormity of the big goal.

FORMULA 2: Finish the most important tasks and stop wasting time on irrelevant activities.

To be an effective time user, you must make sure you are spending your time on only what is important. Don't waste time on irrelevant activities that add no value to your life. Choose what's important and use your time to achieve it.

FORMULA 3: Determine when you are most effective and energized, then plan your tasks within that time.

We don't all enjoy doing the same tasks at the same time of the day. Some people are more effective and energized when carrying out certain tasks in the day while some others get such energy and effectiveness at night for the same task. Therefore make sure you understand when best you are effective and then schedule your most important tasks within that time of the day. If you try to do a task at your odd hours, you will waste so much time only to find out that you did a poor job after all.

FORMULA 4: Set very few priorities and adhere to them.

We live in a world where people are always busy but produce little or no results. People simply do not have priorities and tend to do too many things unproductively. If you desire to be productive with your time, you should select a maximum of two things that are your highest priority, and plan time to work on them.

FORMULA 5: Turn down things that are inconsistent with your priorities.

It is no use setting priorities if you won't stick to them. Most people after setting priorities still get distracted by all the irrelevant activities beckoning on the use of their time. In life friends and family are going to demand the use of your time with you, most times for low yielding activities. This means that if you really want to be an effective time manager you will have to learn to say no to other people and do so frequently.

FORMULA 6: Schedule time for the focused effort.

The best way to effectively use time is to schedule it. Whatever you have chosen to be your priority, set a time to it and be focused on achieving it. Schedule time every day to work on just one thing. Lose no time; be always employed in something useful; cut off all unnecessary actions."

FORMULA 7: Always improve on the things you do better and faster.

People who have become great like Benjamin Franklin only became great because they learned how to invest time into improving whatever it is they were called to do. In order to gain mastery over whatever you have been called to do, you must look for ways of improving how you do them. This involves investing time into repeated rehearsals and consistent practice.

Dear friends, I believe it is obvious from the foregoing that Benjamin Franklin understood the importance of time management and thanks to that, he became great. No man can achieve the successes he achieved if he didn't first know the value of time. Greatness is born out of proper time management. You could see from his quote below that he never wasted his time because he knew that time is life and life are time.

> *"Dost thou love life? Then do not squander time, for that's the stuff that life is made of."*
> BENJAMIN FRANKLIN

The fact that Benjamin Franklin became great because he understood the power of time conversion could be seen in his scientific achievements. He invested most of his time into researching science by constantly experimenting until science experiments became a hobby for him. The following were his achievements in science.

1. Franklin stove — a wood-burning stove for distributing heat throughout a room.

2. His famous experiment of kite and key in the thunderstorm that proved that lightning and electricity were one and the same thing.

3. His understanding of the nature of charges made him the first person to give electricity positive and negative charges.

4. The first flexible urinary catheter.

5. Glass harmonica.

6. Bifocal glasses.

7. He was credited with the idea of daylight saving time.

There was no way a man could have achieved so much if he didn't invest time into adding value to himself. It is clear that he became great because he used his time properly. You also must learn to value time if you must become great like Benjamin Franklin. I encourage you to apply the time management formulas above to your life so that through them you can buy greatness.

HOW TO EXCHANGE YOUR LIFE FOR GREATNESS

Most people do not know how to exchange their lives for eternal treasures. I am going to be showing you how to do it. I am going to reveal to you the secrets of living your life for greatness. Every great person that ever existed knew this secret I am about to reveal to you. They knew that in order to become great, one must understand the secret of time conversion. They all understood that the only instrument through which time could be converted to yield greatness is the instrumentality of work. When I say work, I don't mean job. I don't mean going to mortgage your life for salary. I am talking about work just as an instrument of conversion. I am talking about using work as the avenue for converting time to whatever you want. Once the great men and women in history understood that work could be used to convert time, they all converted their time into what they needed to have. And what they chose to have was greatness. They rather preferred to be great than to live in mediocrity. They could only afford to live a life of greatness. They could not afford the vanity of living a mundane life. They knew that their lives were given to them to fulfill great purposes. They understood that life should only be exchanged for something that is valuable and not for mundane things like houses and cars. They knew that if you could get greatness that greatness will give you cars later on. Not just cars, greatness will give you as many houses you desire. Greatness will give you as much money as you want.

If you will exchange your life for greatness, if you will use the currency of time to buy greatness; then greatness will deliver to you every other thing you need in life This means that if there is anything you need in life that you haven't gotten, it is because you are yet to pay for it via the currency of time. You can have anything you need in life. The only price you have to pay is for you to exchange your life for greatness and greatness will deliver that thing you need to you. You only have to pay the currency of time and you can buy greatness and everything else.

You can exchange your life for greatness instead of for cars. You can invest your life for memorable things of eternal value instead of for houses. You can invest your life for a great future instead of for food and perishable things. I want to teach you how not to live your life for vanity and emptiness. So the question is how do you do it?

You must remember that everything is bought by the currency of time like I have said before. Just mention any great person that you know or let's look at the life of Michelangelo for instance. How did he get that greatness? He knew that time is life and that time is passing automatically. He understood that whether you use time or not it keeps passing by naturally. So he decided to use time. He couldn't afford to allow time just waste away like that. He had to convert the passing time into something. He developed the habit of converting every time that passes into products. This is a trait common to all great people as was also true for Benjamin Franklin. They know that every minute of time that passes must be converted into something. You must intercept the passing time else it will fly away into vanity. You must have heard the cliché "Time waits for nobody" It is true that time is always in a hurry to pass by and until you use it to produce something, it hurries away and it is gone. Michelangelo understood this truth about time and thanks to it, he became great.

DO YOU KNOW MICHELANGELO?

Michelangelo Buonarroti was born on March 6, 1475, in Caprese, Italy. His father used to beat him because he didn't do his lessons but drew all the time. He didn't want the boy to become an artist. He considered an artist's trade to be beneath the family dignity. But finally, since Michelangelo was so stubborn, he apprenticed him (1488) to a painter (Ghirlandaio), who afterward claimed to have taught him all he knew.

Michelangelo was exceptionally good at drawing and copying things. He impressed everyone with his version of an engraving by a German artist (Schongauer).

Michelangelo learned about sculpture (1489) at a school set up in the palace of a rich and powerful duke named Lorenzo de Medici. After only a few days he surprised Lorenzo with a perfect stone copy of a faun. Lorenzo invited him to live in his palace, gave him a place at his table, and a violet robe to wear. He lived there for three years and, while carving his first works in marble, sat in classes with Lorenzo's sons, taught by the great teachers (Humanists) of Florence.

From the story above, I want us to consider a few things about Michelangelo that made him great. The first thing we could notice about him was that he had a passion and love for drawings. He would rather draw pictures than solving his assignments at school. That was a pointer to what he was born to do. The second thing which was the most striking thing about him was that he drew all the time. He converted most of his time into drawing and perfecting his skills and talent in the world of art. Michelangelo was exceptionally good at drawing because he invested most of his time to learn and perfect the act of drawing. There is no great person in history who gained mastery in a particular skill without first investing so much time into perfecting that skill.

Because he converted his time into added value to himself, he became so good that he was invited to the palace of Lorenzo. Only a man who is exceptionally skillful can stand before kings. Only men who have invested time to become the best in what they do are fit to sit and dine with great men. Whatever it is you have been called to do, if you will invest time into perfecting it, you will soon be reckoned among the great in your society.

Lorenzo de Medici suddenly became sick and died (1492). Lorenzo's successor, his son Piero, kept Michelangelo at the palace and ordered him to make a snowman. Michelangelo made his first trip to the quarries of Carrara to get the marble for his next great statue, the *Pietà*.

Florence became a republic (they executed Savonarola) and Michelangelo went back home. He sculpted a marble Cupid (1495) and treated it to look old. A crooked merchant sold it as an antique to a Cardinal in Rome. When he found out, the Cardinal returned the Cupid to the agent. He did not blame Michelangelo but he didn't keep this statue either. He invited Michelangelo to live at his palace in Rome and commissioned a life-sized statue of Bacchus, the God of wine.

Michelangelo returned to Florence to try to get a big marble block that was being handed out by the city governor. It had been standing around in a yard for years and had a hole through it, so it was considered worthless. He took measurements and designed for it a statue of David, the shepherd boy who killed Goliath with a stone from his sling. David is seventeen feet high. Michelangelo carved it in just eighteen months and it was set up in front of the Town Hall (Palazzo Della Signoria) of Florence.

Julius II, as soon as he was elected Pope (1505), wanted to do great things and called Michelangelo to Rome to design and build his tomb. Michelangelo came up with a complex design with forty statues, which delighted the Pope. In great spirits, Michelangelo went to Carrara to quarry the marble. He returned after eight months and set up shop near the Vatican. The Pope used to drop by his workshop to chat and see how things were coming along. Suddenly the Pope changed his mind about the tomb and canceled the project. Michelangelo was so shocked and angered that he destroyed his models, left Rome by night, and went back home to Florence (1506).

THE CEILING OF THE SISTINE CHAPEL

Then Julius called Michelangelo to Rome to paint the ceiling of the Sistine Chapel (1508). "But I'm not a painter," Michelangelo protested. He had painted very little and the Pope was asking him to fill three thousand square feet of ceiling. Julius wouldn't take no for an answer. Painting the ceiling of the Sistine Chapel took four years and was the hardest thing Michelangelo ever did. He worked alone, pushing himself to the limit every day. He ate old bread and slept in his work clothes. "I have no time for friends," he wrote his father. "And I hope the Pope will pay me soon because I haven't got a penny left."

When the ceiling was only half-finished, the impatient Pope ordered Michelangelo to take down the scaffolding and open the chapel to the public. The paintings created a great stir in Rome and all Italy. They illustrated the saga of Man from his creation to the coming of Christ.

Pope Clement ordered him to paint the altar wall of the Sistine Chapel. It took him eight years to finish *The Last Judgment* (1541) because of interruptions for other work and illness. He fell off the scaffold once and was in bed for months. It was his last great painting. But when he was over seventy he did two more huge frescoes in the Vatican: the *Conversion of St. Paul* and the *Crucifixion of St. Peter*.

At last, he finished the Julius Tomb. In fact, most of it was sculpted by his helpers. But the central figure — the Moses — is one of Michelangelo's most powerful statues.

The last important job he had, which occupied him for years when he was old, was St. Peter's Basilica. Two Popes made him the official architect. An assistant helped him build a model for the dome.

He left a lot of unfinished statues around in Rome and Florence. One, the *Duomo Pietá* he intended for his own grave but became unsatisfied with it and smashed it to pieces.

He worked on another — the *Rondanini Pietá* — almost until the day he died.

He died at 89 (1564) after a few days with a fever. His nephew took his body back home to Florence. The funeral was one of the biggest Florence ever saw. More than a hundred artists attended.

Dear friends, there was no way Michelangelo could achieve such greatness if he was not hardworking. His works were masterpieces and everyone who saw them were mesmerized by them. People were wowed by his artistic paintings because they were just wonderful. However, he became a master of his skills only because he worked so hard. I said earlier that the instrument through which time is converted is called work. It was thanks to hard work that Michelangelo became great. You could see that he was very hardworking in his days as attested to by one of his quotes below.

*"If people knew how hard I had to work
to gain my mastery, it would not seem so
wonderful at all."*
MICHELANGELO BUONARROTI

So, dear friends, if you really desire greatness, you should make up your mind to be a hard worker. You should learn to convert your time into tangible products through the instrumentality of work like Michelangelo did. You can gain the mastery over any skill if only you will invest time to work hard on it. Instead of wasting your time with friends and on social media, why not convert it to greatness? Michelangelo didn't surround himself with friends because he had no time for friends, he lived in isolation fulfilling his purpose by converting his time into developing his skills. He spent months and years working on several projects that the world celebrated him for. If you want to be great, you must learn the secret of great men. They all understood the power of time conversion.

THE FIRST PRINCIPLE OF GREATNESS

The first thing you want to do to become great is to discover your area of calling. The secret of all greatness is to discover what you were born to do in life and then do it. You must find out your gifts and talents. For Michelangelo, he discovered that his own gift was in drawing artworks. He was able to answer the first question for the journey of life; the question of "**What** on earth am I her for?" When you want to become great, you have to know what to do. I mean you must first determine what you were born to do. To answer the question of "What?" you must discover your gifts and talents. Your gifts, talents, and calling will help you to know what you must do. So in my own case, I want to raise reformers. I want to raise great men and transform nations. For Michelangelo, he needed to paint. It is your gifting and talents that dictate to you what to do. It was his talent that gave him direction as to what to do with his life. Therefore you must find out what talents and gifting you have and that will help you answer the question of "What?" You cannot answer the question "What?" without discovering who you are. Michelangelo answered that question by discovering that he was gifted at painting and drawing. Therefore self-discovery is the key to knowing what to do with your life. The starting point for greatness is to know what to do with your life.

The second question you must answer to become great is the question of "When?" Michelangelo also answered that question. "**When?**" answers the question of time and that is the key, that is the currency. He understood that every minute and second of his time will fly away if he didn't convert it. He had to convert every passing time into products. He knew that as time passes by, his life passes by too. He knew that as time diminishes, life diminishes too. He, however, didn't want his life to just diminish with time. He had to answer the question of when by making sure that "**Now**" is the time. He knew the danger of procrastinating his greatness for later. He understood that before **later** comes, a lot of time would have been lost. So he made sure he converted the maximum amount of time that passes by in the day because he knew that passing time was actually his life passing by. He had to make use of every minute of his time when he was not sleeping. Every second and minute that you are not sleeping should be converted, investing your life and your time into doing that thing that you were born to do.

Dear friends, as I bring this chapter to a close, I want us to summarize the interesting facts that we have learned from this chapter. The first thing is that everybody has the potential to become great. But what is greatness? Greatness is the amount of time you were able to invest into cultivating your ground. Greatness is the quality of time you are able to invest into your purpose. It is the quality of time you are able to convert into the production of value. The quality of time you are able to concentrate and use to produce values is what determines your greatness. That was why Benjamin Franklin and Michelangelo became great men in history. They understood time conversion. The second thing we learned from this chapter is that without work, time cannot be converted and it will waste away. Therefore to be truly great, begin to convert all your passing time into products through hard work. Such hard work was displayed by Michelangelo and Benjamin Franklin and thanks to it, they became great. You too can buy greatness by converting your time into greatness through hard work. The third thing you must not forget is that all the great men in history as seen from our examples in this chapter discovered their purpose in life and invested their time into fulfilling it. You can never truly become great if you do not discover your purpose in life. Therefore strive to discover why you exist and then begin to invest your time into your purpose and calling. Begin to convert your time into added value to yourself and to others. Find out your talents and gifting and invest your whole time into perfecting them and becoming the best of yourself.

I believe this chapter was inspiring and educating to you. I want to encourage you to proceed to the next chapter as I show you practical ways to getting the best out of your time and how you can become great through the power of time conversion.

TIME PRINCIPLES
FROM CHAPTER ONE

1. Everybody potentially can be great. It is not only some few people who could be great.

2. It is rather your limitation that decides to what extent of greatness and to what height you are going to arise in this life. Your level of promotion in life is determined by how much you know.

3. There is indeed no limitation in life to anybody's height of greatness. The only limitation that we all have is the limitation that we create for ourselves.

4. There is no one who was supposed to come to this world and leave empty.

5. You are not supposed to be here in this world and not leave something for which you could be called great.

6. Greatness is not greater than you. You have total control over greatness. You can decide to be great and it will happen.

7. The key to your greatness is under your control. You are the one in charge of your life and how great you become is up to you.

8. All I am saying is that you should begin to see greatness as something you cannot do without. Begin to see greatness as something that you cannot afford not to have.

9. You can leave your mark. You can do something remarkable with your life. You have what it takes to leave your footprint in the sand of history.

10. It is unpardonable for you to leave this world without recording some greatness in your account.

HOW TO BECOME GREAT
THROUGH TIME CONVERSION

1. Greatness is an attainment that is bought with the currency of time.

2. People who have become great have only become great because they bought that greatness. They purchased that greatness but only through the currency of time.

3. It is the time that delivers greatness to people. Therefore if you can know how to convert your time by investing it, then you can buy greatness with it.

4. Your life is not meant to be used in exchange for mundane things like houses and cars but to purchase greatness.

5. It is the quality of time you are able to convert into the production of value. The quality of time you are able to concentrate and use to produce values is what determines your greatness.

6. To be truly great, begin to convert all your passing time into products. Begin to invest your time into your purpose and calling.

7. Find out your talents and gifting and invest your whole time into perfecting them and becoming the best of yourself.

8. In order to become great, one must understand the secret of time conversion.

9. The secret of all greatness is to discover what
   you were born to do in life and then do it.
   You must find out your gifts and talents.

10. Greatness is the amount of time you were
    able to invest into cultivating your ground.
    Greatness is the quality of time you are
    able to invest into your purpose.

CHAPTER 2

WHAT DO YOU DO WITH YOUR TIME?

In this first chapter, we explained the principles of greatness with which men like Benjamin Franklin and Michelangelo became great. The criteria for greatness was said to be dependent on how much time each person is able to convert into added value and products in one's area of calling and purpose. In this chapter. I hereby want to tell you what to do with your time in order to attain greatness. I am about to challenge you to greatness in this session by bringing to your awareness the principles of time conversion that will help you better utilize your time. Read on dear friends!

Have you ever felt bored? Have you ever wondered what you could do with your time? I believe there are times in your life that you were alone all by yourself and didn't know what to do. You probably would have attended some meetings in which you felt like you were wasting your time because nothing of worth was achieved from that meeting. There could have been moments in your life that you had enough time in your hands but didn't know what to do with it. I am going to show you exactly what you should do with your time to make it productive.

Most people on the face of the earth do not know what to do with their time. A greater percentage of people on the earth have at one point in their life had a lot of time in their hands but squandered it unknowingly. The reason for this wastage is simply because people do not know what to do with their time. The majority of people on earth are ignorant of what their time should be used for.

Unfortunately, that is how most of us have treated time — our life!!! We have just all of a sudden discovered that here we are, with something called time seemingly precious, but not deeply appreciated. So we end up treating it the way we deem fit.

Let me ask you these questions. How have you been treating time? What do you do with your time when you are alone? The question most people do not ask themselves is what they could do with their time to make it productive. Even those who are jobless do not know how to best use the free time that they have. That is why you trivialize time when you don't know what do. The difference between one person who is living in poverty and another person living in wealth is their understanding of what to do with time. The reason why one man is great and another man is living in mediocrity is simply because one understood the value of time while the other did not. Haven't you seen two children of the same parents who grew up in the same house and attended the same school but with one of them rising to become a voice in society while the other is just struggling to make a living? What is the difference? It is their understanding of time. One knew what to do with his time while the other did not.

Another consequence of not knowing the value of what you possess in this case the value of time is that there would be some other people around you that will better understand what you possess. While you are playing Candy Crush and Criminal case games with your time, they will keep using their time for studying and investing in their lives. It won't be long before the difference between them and you will surface. In the nearest future, those who understood the value of time will rule over those who trivialized time.

Even though all men were created equal, it is, however, tragic to see some men rise to stardom while others are never heard about throughout their lifetime and they just die ordinary without leaving a mark in their generation. The reason for this difference between people is simply because some people do not know what to do with time. Even though God has given the gift of time to all men equally, it is what each man does with this equal gift of time that determines whether or not he will be great.

What do you do with your time when you are not in school? What do you do with your time when you are not in the office? What do you do with your time when you have a whole day doing nothing? You see, I can go on and on asking these questions but I want you to check your life for the past five, ten, maybe twenty years of your life. What have you been doing with your time? Can you show me something tangible that you have done with your time?

Every one of us must be able to answer these questions. You must know what to do with your time if you must become great in this life. You must know what to do with your time if you must fulfill your purpose on the earth. It is a pity that every one of us desires greatness yet not many of us know what to do with our time. Every one of us must learn how to make our time productive. You and I must learn and understand the value of time and how to invest it if we must achieve anything of worth in our lifetime.

THE FIRST PRINCIPLE OF TIME

The first and general principle of time is that TIME MUST BE CONVERTED INTO PRODUCTS! That is what you should do with your time. Convert it to products. The time comes in seconds. The time comes in minutes and in hours. You must not think that time comes in years or months. You must view time as coming in seconds and minutes and at most in hours or days. This view of time creates a more sense of urgency of time than viewing time as passing in months or years.

> *"The quickest way to run out of time is to think you have enough of it."*
> STEWART STAFFORD

If you must make your time productive, then begin to view time in its most urgent form; in seconds and in minutes. When you view time in months or years, you begin to think you have enough of it and before you know it, you have lost all the time. Have you ever postponed some tasks because you thought you had enough time only to find out that you later ran out of time and couldn't accomplish those task? That is the danger of procrastination; it gives you a fake impression that you have all the time and makes you forget that time passes by every second and minute. When I say time must be converted, what I am saying is that seconds must be converted. Minutes must be converted. Hours must be converted and days must be converted. Now, what do I mean by this! I mean that to know what to do with time is to convert a day and to convert a day is to produce a product. Therefore to measure your time management you must access yourself by how many products you were able to produce on that particular day, or how many products you were able to produce in that particular hour, a minute or second.

The secret of all greatness is in knowing what to do with time. The secret of all the great men and women in history is that they converted their time into tangible products. Greatness is only possible thanks to the products you are able to produce per seconds, per minutes, per hour and per day. Is there any valuable product you can account for as produced per hour of your life daily? Ok! Do you have anything tangible to show for the last one week of your life? If you have no products, then you have not been converting your time. Since time comes in seconds, in minutes and in hours, we must learn to convert time else it will slip away and can never be regained. To be effective and productive is to not squander time and to live a life of understanding and wisdom, is to not waste time. Ask yourself these questions; have I been squandering time? Have I been wasting time? Do I have products to show for my past seconds, minutes, and hours and days?

ELON MUSK SUCCESS STORY

Elon Musk (22 in 1993) read 10 hours a day, both science fiction and non-fiction. By 4th grade, he was reading the *Encyclopedia Britannica*. Musk was frustrated with slow formal classroom learning and did most of his learning through reading.

Elon Reeve Musk was born on June 28, 1971, in Pretoria, South Africa. He was the oldest of three children. His father is a South African-born British and engineer Errol Musk, and his mother is a Canadian-English and dietetics expert Maye Musk. Musk spent his childhood in South Africa and at the age of 9, he got his first personal computer, the Commodore VIC-20. Elon immediately got interested in programming and started to learn it by himself. At the age of 12, he earned $500 by selling a computer game Blastar (a shooter similar to Space Invaders), which he had created by himself.

The reason for Elon Musk's success could be seen in the first line of this success story "Elon Musk read 10 hours every day" That is the difference between him and his contemporaries. His understanding of time conversion at an early age is the primary reason for his success in life. The dividing line between those who will be great and those who will be mediocre is the amount of time each person converts into added value to himself. How many African children do you know who read as much as 10 hours every day? Even adults in Nigeria can hardly invest such an amount of time daily into reading and research in the library and laboratory yet every one of them wants to be great and wealthy. Nigerians would rather waste time in church services, at the sport viewing centers and at home sleeping or watch Nigerian movies. It is a pity that our country may not be able to raise inventors and innovators if this attitude of time wastage is not corrected. It is for this reason that I am pouring out my heart if I could at least provoke you and many others who will read this book to greatness by teaching you the principles of greatness through time conversion.

You could notice that by 4th grade, Elon Musk already started reading the Encyclopaedia Britannica and at age 9 he was already into computer programming which he learned by himself and sold his first video game at age 12. Only a child who understood time conversion could achieve such success at such an early age. Elon Musk constantly added value to himself investing his time into voracious reading.

After graduating from a secondary school in Pretoria, he decided to leave his home, and, without the support of his parents, to immigrate to the United States. However, he did not get into the United States right away.

In 1989, Elon Musk moved to Canada to the relatives of his mother. Having obtained a Canadian citizenship, Elon went to Montreal. At first, he worked in low paid jobs and almost a year was teetering on the brink of poverty. At the age of 19, he entered Queens University in Kingston, Ontario. Elon Musk has been studying in Ontario for two years and then, finally, his dream came true — in 1992, he relocated to the United States. He was able to move to the US after receiving a scholarship from The University of Pennsylvania. He earned his Bachelor of Science degree in Physics Bachelor the next year, but decided to continue his studying at The Wharton School of the University of Pennsylvania for one more year and obtained a Bachelor of Science degree in Economics as well.

Musk figured out that humanity had to expand the limits of its consciousness to learn to ask the right questions; and he had found his question: what things would have the great impact on the future of humanity's destiny? Elon Musk decided that those would be the internet, the transition to renewable energy sources, and space colonization. He wanted to try to contribute in all three of them.

"When I was in college, I wanted to be involved in things that would change the world."

ELON MUSK

HIS FIRST TWO COMPANIES

In the summer of 1995, Elon Musk made the second and the most important decision in his life. Having graduated from the University of Pennsylvania, he enrolled in the graduate school at Stanford University to pursue studies in the field of applied physics and materials science. However, after 2 days, he left the graduate school and together with his brother, Kimbal Musk, he created his first IT Company Zip2. He worked from early morning until late evening. He lived in the same warehouse where he rent the office, and when he needed to take a shower he had to go to locker rooms of a local stadium. In return, he accumulated savings and kept the company afloat during the most difficult first two years.

At that moment, the Internet was experiencing a period of rapid growth and development; however, nobody had ever earned a considerable fortune on it. Musk's company was one of the first ones to do this: he created a platform where newspapers — including credible ones as New York Times — could offer their customers some additional commercial services.

In 1999, the biggest search engine of that time AltaVista (later acquired by Compaq) bought Zip2 for $307 million in cash and $34 million in securities. This deal set a record for selling a company for cash. Musk spent $20 million on a 1,800-square-foot condominium and completely renovated it.

In 1999, Musk started to work on electronic payment systems that were gaining popularity. The X.com startup became his new business. In March 2000, X.com merged with a rival company Confinity. In 2001, after the merger, X.com was renamed to PayPal and Elon Musk became the chairman and chief executive of PayPal.

Musk was involved in the development of new business models, conducted a successful viral marketing campaign, which led to a rapid increase in a number of customers. In 2002, eBay bought PayPal for $1.5 billion. Elon Musk received $180 million for his share from PayPal and had enough funds to pursue his other interests: space engineering and alternative energy sources.

Dear friends, it is obvious from the success story of Elon Musk that he was an investor of time. He invested so much time into what he was born to do. He first discovered that he could contribute to humanity in such a way that could change the world for good. With such mentality, he began to be purposeful with every minute of his time that passes. He knew that to change the world, he would of necessity be above his contemporaries in innovative ideas, knowledge, and wisdom. He also knew that the possibility of such dreams of changing the world could only be realized by properly investing time into learning. No wonder he could get a degree in physics and later on in economics. We could see a studious spirit in him and that is one of the secrets of great men. They know how to convert their time into studying and researching. My charge to you and to anyone else who desire greatness is that you should not trivialize time. Value time and convert it into greatness by investing it into learning and researching all that you can. Is there still anyone in Nigeria who wants to be great? If yes, then go lock up yourself in your room, library or laboratory and study ten hours every day. It won't be long before the whole world will hear of your exploits.

THE ELECTRIC CAR

Musk {CEO of Tesla} participated in designing of their first electric car, which was a Tesla Roadster sports car based on the British Lotus Elise. He insisted on using carbon fiber composite materials in the hull to minimize weight, developed the battery module and even some elements of design, like the headlights. By 2006, the project has got into newspapers and Musk received Global Green 2006 product design award for Tesla Roadster design. Soon, things went smoothly, which was especially impressive against the backdrop of stagnating traditional auto industry. A German multinational automotive corporation Daimler made critical investments of $50 million in Tesla Motors and it helped save the company. Soon, the U.S. Department of Energy authorized the inclusion of Tesla Motors in a pool of innovative transport companies and authorized it to receive a preferential interest-bearing loan.

On June 29, 2010, Tesla Motors started its initial public offering (IPO). It was the second (after Ford) car-manufacturing company in the U.S. history that entered the IPO market. As of February 05, 2015, one share of stock of Tesla Motors, Inc. cost $220.99, and its total market cap. reached $27.44 billion. Elon Musk owns 30% of Tesla Motors, Inc. (TSLA).

The main reason for Tesla's financial success became a premium sedan Tesla Model S, with the battery that supplies 265 miles (426 km) of range in the EPA 5-cycle test. The production of Model S started in June 2012 with a price tag starting at $69,900 and was ranked 99 out of 100 points by Consumer Reports and the highest safety rating from the National Highway Safety Administration, a 5.4 out of 5 points.

At the presentation of Model S, Musk categorically stated that in twenty years, more than half of produced vehicles would be electric ones. Elon Musk believes that the world has become dependent on oil. This dependence leads to climate change and permanent geopolitical tensions. A refusal of internal combustion engines in favor of electric motors can make a difference. Therefore, Tesla Motors is not a mere business for Musk.

If you read the success story of Elon Musk with an undivided attention, you would have noticed that he is a very intelligent and hardworking man. His ideas are revolutionary and could change the course of history. He believes he could make the world a better place by contributing his quota to humanity. All his inventions were only possible thanks to how much time he converted into added value to himself. While you are wasting time on irrelevant things, Elon musk was researching on how he could change the world through science and technology. One of his inventions that could change the world is called SpaceX. It is an aerospace manufacturer and space transport services company founded by Elon musk in the year 2002.

SpaceX's achievements include the first privately funded, liquid-propellant rocket (Falcon 1) to reach orbit, in 2008; the first privately funded company to successfully launch, orbit and recover a spacecraft (Dragon), in 2010; and the first private company to send a spacecraft (Dragon) to the ISS, in 2012. The launch of SES-8, in 2013, was the first SpaceX delivery into geosynchronous orbit, while the launch of the Deep Space Climate Observatory (DSCOVR), in 2015, was the company's first delivery beyond Earth orbit.

It is disheartening to find out that the brain behind all these inventions does not even believe in God. Though he is not a Christian he understands how to invest time into exploring land and space while we who are Christians boast of only how many hours we could spend in church and numerous prayer meetings. The earth belongs to God and he has charged us with the responsibility of replenishing and exploring the earth but it is unfortunate that it is unbelievers and atheists who are doing what we should be doing. It seems to me that the world understands time conversion more the church does. That is why the major inventions in the world are almost all emanating from the world but not the church. My sincere wish is that through this book, you will make a decision to join the list of inventors and people who are making the world a better place. I hope that you will resolve to not be overly religious and earthly useless. Begin to invest your time into research and studies about how you could impact your world positively because only through the proper conversion of time could you become great.

WASTE TIME, SPEND TIME, OR INVEST TIME

Every human being is either wasting time, spending time or investing time.

If you waste time, you don't even get anything for it. You don't get compensated for it at all. You just throw it in the garbage and you don't even know what happened to it at all. Any time that cannot be accounted for is a wasted time. I am sure you can begin to imagine how much of your time that has been unaccounted for. I believe you can see clearly now how much time you have wasted with nothing to show for it. When you sit down doing nothing you are wasting time. When you walk about doing nothing you are wasting time. When you don't know what to do with the time you are wasting time. When there is nothing to do you are wasting time. People who know the value of time are always doing something valuable with their time. If you have no product to show for your time you are a time waster. If you are bored or idle you are a time squanderer. It is impossible to be bored when you have a lot of valuable tasks that you are performing with your time. To just sit down idle and do nothing with time is a waste of time. You can never become great living the life of a time waster.

> *"I would I could stand on a busy corner,*
> *hat in hand, and beg people to throw me*
> *all their wasted hours."*
> BERNARD BERENSON

On the other hand, when you spend time; you at least know what you did with the time. You remember what activity you carried out within that time. You can at least say for example; that was the time you went to work or that was the time you went to the market. You at least could see some compensation for a spent time. You are paid some salaries and wages in exchange for your time spent at work. You are exchanging your time for some peanuts and porridge when you spend your time. You are selling out your life for a little porridge.

When you spend your time you are actually spending your life. Any time that is spent or wasted is a life wasted or spent. Any life wasted or spent is gone and it will never come back. Anybody that does not value time does not value life. Whenever we lose time we are actually losing our life.

Most people on earth are just spending time at work, in school or in church without having anything of value to show for it. Even when you are working and getting some salaries, your life is going and once it's gone you can never get it back. You have wasted it for some little salary. You may have a car or maybe a house or at least something little to show for spending your life but you are still not multiplying your life. You can never become great if you continue to live your life like this.

The only thing you have to show for a wasted or spent time is that you just realize that you are getting older. You only discover that your life is getting finished. You only remember that you went to work, to church or to school. You have no product to show except the fact that you got a job or that you have been going to church for so and so number of years or that you got married so and so number of years ago and that you have children; you are just spending your time doing some mundane things of no eternal value. When you can only remember the mundane things you did but do not have any valuable products to show for your time, then you are a time spender.

However, when you invest your time, you are investing your life. When you invest your life you don't lose it. When you invest your life, you are multiplying it. When you invest your life you reproduce your life. You reproduce your life by reproducing your gifts and your talents. When you reproduce yourself you don't spend your life, you multiply it.

Reproduce yourself and multiply your life. That is why the charge God gave to Adam was "Be fruitful and multiply" The minimum you should do with your life is to at least reproduce it. It is, however, more honorable to multiply your life. When you invest your time, you are pouring your life into others. You are actually reproducing yourself when you invest your life.

When you invest your life, you realize that even though you are getting older, you are also increasing in your products. Products in the form of knowledge, products in the form of added value to yourself and to others, products in the form of perfected skills and talents, products in the form of books written or read, products in the form of songs which were written or musical albums produced. There is no ending to the number of products you can produce with your time if well invested. But for you to be able to be fruitful, to multiply and saturate the earth with your products, you have to first know how to properly use the currency of time. You must know how to invest time. The question therefore is; how can you use the currency of time judiciously? How can you use the currency of time not to just buy car, house or any other mundane thing but to invest time into fulfilling your purpose and calling? To properly invest your time, first find out your calling. Find out your purpose. Find out your gifts and talents. Then invest your time into perfecting them. When you invest your time you will notice that you are being fruitful and that you are multiplying your life. This is so because you are investing your life into your destiny, into your calling and in fulfillment of your purpose. This is a beautiful kind of life, isn't it? This is the kind of life you should be living. I want to show you what to do with your time. The whole essence of this book is to teach you how to live such a life of investment on daily basis. My heart desire is that you learn from this book how to get products daily from your time.

> *"Dost thou love life? Then do not*
> *squander time, for that's the stuff that life*
> *is made of."*
> BENJAMIN FRANKLIN.

What I am talking about is that since life is in time, since life is in seconds, minutes and hours; that means to waste time is to waste life. To lose time is to lose a life. So don't waste time. So when you are just living your mundane life; just walking about or you are just sleeping and waking up and just chatting on the telephone and on social media; you are wasting life. When you are just drinking and clubbing you are wasting life. When you spend your time watching TV programs that add no value to your life, you are wasting life. When you spend two hours every day watching premier league and champions league you are wasting life. Greatness cannot be attained by wasting time on frivolities of life.

"Successful people have libraries.
The rest have big screen TVs"
JIM ROHN

THE PROPER VIEW OF TIME

Let's assume you have all the time now. How then should you live your life so that it's not just wasted or spent? What should you do with your time so that it's well invested? That is what I am about to reveal to you in this session. For you not to waste or spend your life, you must first begin to see time and life correctly. You must first understand that time is life and life is time. To see time and life correctly, you must begin to access life as seconds, as minutes and as hours. You must realize that whenever you waste a second you are wasting life. If you waste a minute you have wasted life and if you waste an hour you have wasted life.

For you to maximize time, you want to make sure that every second of the day that comes is converted into some products. You want to ensure that every minute and hour of the day that passes are being converted into some values. For you to be great, you must learn to convert every second of your life. You must live a life of self-consciousness all the time. You must become conscious of what you are doing per time. You must make sure that every second of your life counts. You will need to invest every bit of your time into your destiny and purpose if you truly desire to be great. If you want to be great you will have to ask yourself; am I wasting time/life right now? Am I spending time/life or am I investing time/life? You must consciously ask yourself; what am I doing now? What consequence is it going to have on my destiny? What product is this going to give me?

What services am I providing? What value am I adding to others? What values am I adding to myself? Am I investing in myself? If you consciously ask yourself these questions daily, you will stop spending or waste time on low yielding activities. You will begin to invest time in only high yielding activities.

> *"Time is the most valuable coin in your life. You and you alone will determine how that coin will be spent. Be careful that you do not let other people spend it for you."*
> CARL SANDBURG

DON'T ALLOW RELIGIOUS MEETINGS STEAL YOUR TIME

The tradition of going to church every day of the week is not an indicator of greatness. Don't think that spending your time in church every day will guarantee you greatness. If that church is not adding value to your life, you may want to reconsider how often you go to church. So the way to control your life is this; every minute you live, maybe you are in church; ask yourself "why am I here? What product am I producing by being here?" I know most Christians just go to church like dummies. Every day of the week they are in church. They are just obeying the traditions of the church and practicing the routine without having value to show for the plenty hours spent in church every day. You should ask yourself "could I use that time for something more productive? Could I use that time to create a product that can add value to humanity?

I know you may be thinking that I am against church attendance. You perhaps are thinking that going to church every day gives glory to God. Let me ask you a question. Are you sure the only way to serve God is to go to church daily? Are you really convinced that spending twenty-four hours in church every day is the only way to glorify God?

Going to church is not the only way to serve God. When you go to church you are supposed to go to church to invest in people or to invest in yourself. But you and I know that most time when we go to church, we don't invest in ourselves. We just go there to just feel good and just while away time to repeat the same thing that you already know.

But what if that three, four or five hours you spend in church every day is converted into something else that can bring more glory to God? For example if you decide to stay at home on this Sunday or weekdays and do your research or go to the library and work on your project, if you perfect your research in the laboratory and discover the cure for cancer for example without going to church every day but having personal relationship with God daily, if you are loving God and growing in Him daily, if you are having fellowship with your family and with your friends within a well- regulated time, but when you need to invest your time into giving birth to a product whether it's Sunday or weekdays you work on your research and discover the solution to the traffic problem in your country or if you are working on a formula that could end the corruption problem in your country or if you discover the cure for Diabetes Mellitus, do you think God will not be more glorified?

Don't you think discovering a breakthrough in medicine or engineering will bring more glory to God than just spending every morning and evening in church? In my opinion, I think that will bring more glory to God than going to church every day for ten years with nothing to show for it.

You are killing your life if you are not converting your time. You are killing your life if you are just going through the traditions and routine of church services with no product to show for it. At least when you spend your time at work you get some salaries, some porridge, and peanuts. But when you waste your time in religious meetings, you get nothing except goose bumps which disappear as soon as you leave the service. You become void of products when you waste your time in religious meetings every day. No wonder Nigeria is void of inventions. No wonder Africa has nothing to show for the many hours we spend in church services. What if we spend all the time we waste in uncountable church services in the laboratory doing research and experimenting? What if we convert the times we spend in unending prayer and deliverance vigils into painstakingly researching science and technology, researching medicine and agriculture? Wouldn't we saturate the earth with inventions? Wouldn't we become a country of inventors and great personalities?

Am I against religious gatherings? No! If there is any church service that you attend and it quickens your purpose and adds value to your life, if that church gives you some insight and understanding and a picture of how to do things better and become a solution provider to the problems of humanity in your country, then you can keep attending such a church. If that church puts fire in you and gives you some ideas on how to fulfil your mission and your purpose faster or if the church makes you to see God's purpose faster and equips you to fulfil your destiny, if you see more into the mind of God and into the spirit of God by attending that church, of course, you have to attend the services but you must leave the church to go practice and implement what you have learnt. If the church is adding more value to you than you would have given yourself at that particular time on your own, that means you are maximizing your time. That means you are working in wisdom. It means you are creating products for your time. I advise you to remain in such a church, otherwise take your leave and go discover how to fulfill God's purpose for your life.

Therefore you have to do comparative analysis. You have to do a value analysis to find out what you should be doing with your time. For example, if you use the time you would have spent in church next Sunday to stay back home and write a whole book. You would have reproduced yourself. You would have multiplied that time instead of wasting or just spending it in the church. You have actually invested that time into creating a product. In such a way, your life begins to create value, it is not just going away, and it is being reproduced in a form of a product. Now you can show the world what you did with your time on Sunday. Your life is being multiplied and it is blessing more people all over the world instead of just wasting or spending it in the church. But if you just go to church every Sunday and every weekday and you can't see what you did with your time you are a time waster. If you have no value to show for your life from the numerous church meetings then there is hardly a possibility that you can become great. It is only a fool that will keep doing the same thing again and again and expect a different result. Don't be a fool. Be wise!

DO A COMPARATIVE ANALYSIS
OF TIME AND EVENTS

Most people waste most of their time attending parties. Others waste their time in clubs and cinemas. The party syndrome is so much in Nigeria that almost every week there is a party in the neighborhood. People just waste their entire life attending parties and having no value to show for it. They do not even know that it is a waste of time to just be found attending all available parties. I have an understanding that time is life and life is time and so I am conscious of every minute of time that passes. It is for this same reason that I hardly go for birthday parties. If I ever go for such parties, it must be that I am indispensable in that party and I will do everything possible to run out of that party as soon as possible. Because I am thinking, what value is this party adding to my life? What value can I produce comparatively? What value could I be producing this within this time? Had I used this time I am spending in this party now to read books, I would have added to myself more values. If I spent that time to study, I would have increased my knowledge.

So you must always do a value comparison. You must begin to live your life this way doing a comparative analysis between any two events in your life and making sure you are only investing your time into that event which adds more value to your life. You must always be conscious of your time. What if you spent that time to write, to research, to bless other people, to give to other people, to teach other people? You would have created more values for yourself than just wasting it in a party. You would have reproduced yourself in others instead of wasting your life and your time.

The way to maximize your time is to always ask yourself the questions above, it is to always be in the here and now. It is not to just be everywhere at all times. You must stop living an abstract life. You must stop living like Oh! Today is another day, I don't even know what to do today! Oh! It's night already Oh! I didn't even know that time has gone Oh! You see that is the life of an animal. You are not an animal. You are supposed to be Homo sapiens and Homo sapiens is the thinking man. Humans are supposed to evaluate their lives. You are supposed to give an account of your time and your life on daily basis. Even the bible says you should maximize your time because the time is short.

"He who every morning plans the transactions of that day and follows that plan carries a thread that will guide him through the labyrinth of the most busy life."
VICTOR HUGO

As I bring this chapter to a close, I want you to remember that the first principle of time is that it must be converted into products. Every day of your life must be converted to some products. Invest your time into research and studies like Elon Musk did. You must create value chains for yourself on daily basis. You must know what to do with each passing time. You must plan out your time if you don't want to waste it. Do not become a religious time waster, become an innovator who will invest his time into impacting the world for good.

To further learn how to measure your life and your time, I encourage you to proceed to the next chapter as I teach you how to make your time productive.

TIME PRINCIPLES
FROM CHAPTER TWO

1. The first and general principle of time is that TIME MUST BE CONVERTED INTO PRODUCTS!

2. The difference between one person who is living in poverty and another person living in wealth is their understanding of what to do with time.

3. The reason why one man is great and another man is living in mediocrity is simply because one understood the value of time while the other did not.

4. In the nearest future, those who understood the value of time will rule over those who trivialized time.

5. God has given the gift of time to all men equally. What each man does with this equal gift of time determines whether or not he will be great.

6. You and I must learn and understand the value of time and how to invest it if we must achieve anything of worth in our lifetime.

7. You must view time as coming in seconds and minutes and at most in hours or days. This view of time creates a more sense of urgency of time than viewing time as passing in months or years.

8. Anybody that does not value time does not value life. Whenever we lose time we are actually losing our life.

9. Any time that cannot be accounted
for is a wasted time.

10. You can never become great living
the life of a time waster.

HOW TO BECOME GREAT
THROUGH TIME CONVERSION

1. The secret of all greatness is in knowing what to do with time. The secret of all the great men and women in history is that they converted their time into tangible products.

2. You must know what to do with your time if you must become great in this life. You must know what to do with your time if you must fulfill your purpose on the earth.

3. Therefore to measure your time management you must access yourself by how many products you were able to produce on that particular day, or how many products you were able to produce in that particular hour, a minute or second.

4. Greatness is only possible thanks to the products you are able to produce per seconds, per minutes, per hour and per day.

5. To be effective and productive is to not squander time and to live a life of understanding and wisdom, is to not waste time.

6. Man will always waste time if there is no system to check and compel him to invest his time. But if you must be great you must learn to check and compel yourself to invest time.

7. Since life is in time, since life is in seconds, minutes and hours; that means to waste time is to waste life. To lose time is to lose a life. So don't waste time!

8. For you not to waste or spend your life, you must first begin to see time and life correctly. You must first understand that time is life and life is time.

9. You must realize that whenever you waste a second you are wasting life. If you waste a minute you have wasted life and if you waste an hour you have wasted life.

10. For you to maximize time, you want to make sure that every second of the day that comes is converted into some products. You want to ensure that every minute and hour of the day that passes are being converted into some values. For you to be great, you must learn to convert every second of your life.

CHAPTER 3

HOW TO MEASURE YOUR LIFE

Dear friends, I am glad you made it through to the third chapter of this book. I do hope you still remember all that you read in the first two chapters about how to attain greatness. We said that greatness can only be attained through time conversion. You also saw in the preceding chapters that it is through hard work that time could be converted into greatness as was attested to by the lifestyles of Benjamin Franklin, Michelangelo, and Elon Musk. Having also said in the last chapter that time should be invested instead of wasting or just spending it, I now invite you to read this chapter with keen interest and undivided focus as I reveal to you practical steps to making your time productive. The first thing you need to know in order to properly measure your time is that you must not delay.

DO NOT DELAY!

"If you defer investing your time and energy until you see that you need to, chances are it will already be too late."

CLAYTON M. CHRISTENSEN

Most people do not invest their time because they do not see the need to do that. For example, the system of schooling in Nigerian universities is such that you go to school for about four months and then you write exams at the end of the semester. Most students do not invest their time into studying thoroughly and acquiring knowledge daily but wait until it's a week or two to exams date before they hurriedly want to study everything they have been taught since the beginning of the semester. The end result of such attitude is that they realize that the workload has suddenly become too overwhelming than they could exhaust. The final outcome is that such students fail the exams or manage to pass with an average grade.

However, the students who invested their time daily to study whatever they've been taught by investing their time in the library and doing thorough research end up becoming the best students during exams.

In the Ukraine for example, the system of study in the universities is different from that in Nigeria. The students are made to study and write modules almost every week especially in the medical universities. This approach has helped a lot of students invest their time into studying daily instead of wasting their time and waiting until the end of semester exams before they could study. But the deception of our school system worldwide is that when schools are on holidays, students no longer see the need to study. Instead of investing time, time is being wasted by most students. In fact, most students waste their lives during the holidays. What does that suggest to you? It simply suggests that people do not know what to do with their lives if there is no school system to compel them to invest time into studying.

It means that man will always waste time if there is no system to check and compel him to invest his time. But if you must be great you must learn to check and compel yourself to invest time. If you are waiting to be compelled before you could invest your time productively then it means you are not the owner of your life but the system that is compelling you.

If you waste your time you are wasting your life. If you allow any minute of your time to pass without converting it into products, you will soon realize that you just wasted a part of your life.

Let me tell you my story. I just somehow knew intuitively that my life was supposed to produce some measurable tangible products. I kind of sensed that I must do something with my life and I think every human being is sensing that too. I think every human being probably knows in their subconscious mind that they would like to do something great with their lives. I think everybody knows that and feels that they would like to live a life of value, they would like their lives to be meaningful. They would like their lives to bring forth some results. They would like their lives to be of benefit to humankind somehow.

When I was in my twenties, I use to measure my life by every year that passes. So I would say "today is my twenty-third birthday for example, and I would want to do something between this birthday and my next birthday when I would be twenty-four years old". I wanted to see the products my life would produce within that year. So that was a good start for me. I did that to measure what my life would be able to produce within a year. When that year was over, I would search hard to find if I actually produced any products. I would search hard because I wasn't really purposeful about producing any results. I was just hoping something good would happen. So I will try to remember if anything good actually happened. After the long search, I would rarely find something to hold on to and then I would thank God for at least having something to show for that one year. Maybe I was able to read books or move from one class to a higher class. I even used to measure my life by saying thank God I am still a Christian at least after one year. Foolishness! I was just foolish. I had no real products to show. No proof of my life. I just spent a year and I couldn't even have anything to point to as a product and the highest thing I could point to is that I was still a Christian. A whole year just passed and all I could say was just that I was promoted from the second year to the third year or that I finished my first degree which is just automatic.

I never knew that was just a cheap life. To automatically be promoted from one class to another without any serious self- discipline, and self- improvement is a cheap life. I didn't even have to do anything serious. To Just wake up in the morning, take your bath and go to class every day and get promoted at the end of the year is just an automatic event. That's no product! That is just rubbish. A product is supposed to be what you are intentionally producing with your life at least every month. It is not something you just get by waking up in the morning and sleeping at night every day.

You have not intentionally produced anything with your life if all you have to show after one year is just how you got promoted from one class to another. That is too cheap a product. It means you didn't convert your time into producing valuable products. It means you didn't invest your time into your purpose. It means you allowed your life to diminish without reproducing it. It means your life keeps on reducing, your life keeps on pouring out and you are not converting it to tangible products. It is being wasted or being spent away without any product to show for it. That is a total waste of life.

I didn't have any results to show for my life. It was just a wasteful life. My life used to be just like that until I began to think more and grow more and discover more about life. That was the point when I got to a place where I intentionally made sure that I really produced something with my life within a year. So I began to measure my life with the tangible products I was able to produce within a year.

So the question I have for you is that, do you have any products that you could point to every year of your life or maybe the products you produced last year? Do you have something to point at as the products that your life has produced and not just has produced automatically but intentionally? I am not talking about getting pregnant and producing children. Dogs can produce children. Cats can produce children. That is not what I am talking about. I am talking about what you as a human being is intentionally and purposefully producing with your time. I am talking about a goal that you have set, attained, and the result you could show for it. If you do not have tangible products to show then you may want to reconsider what you do with your time.

HOW I MEASURED MY PRODUCTS

To summarize my story, at the age of twenty-five, I started producing concrete results and concrete fruits. I had concrete products that I could show before my next birthday as what my life could produce and I used to be very happy. I used to be so happy that I didn't live in vain. At least I could see what my life could produce. Even though it was not big enough for anybody to see, even though it was not big enough to be a great achievement, though it was not something that I could be proud of, yet I could see it myself, I saw something that I did with my time. I saw something that my life produced within one year by myself. That brought great joy to me.

Then I kept on maturing and striving, adding value to myself and getting myself educated until I got to a place where I could now measure my life and to gauge it and direct it and actually organize my life in such a way that I have a product to show for every year of my life. But it suddenly dawned on me that I could intentionally set a goal, a target to have a product and a result to show for my life within a year. I just discovered that eh! Instead of producing this result and just waiting, rejoicing and hoping till the following year before producing another result, if I become more purposeful like this and pursue more, and strive more and work hard, maybe I could actually have two products in a year. So I graduated from having one product to show for a year spent on earth to having two products in a year. That means for every six months of my life I had a product. For another six months of my life, I had another product. That was another stage of my life when I could show two products that my life produced within a year. I graduated further to producing three products within a year. I graduated yet again to producing four products in a year. This is a proof that you can do better than you are doing right now. You can improve yourself and become a better investor of time. Do not be satisfied with little successes when you can actually do better.

WHERE ARE THE PRODUCTS OF YOUR LIFE?

I would love to at this juncture ask you this question. **Where are the products of your life?** Have you actually started living a productive life yet? Is there anything you could point to as your products, apart from the instinctive things of life like sleeping with a woman and getting her pregnant and she just gives birth to children? Like I said before, every dog can get pregnant, every cow can get pregnant. I am not talking about instinctive things that just work out by the law of nature. I am talking about concrete fruits, concrete results. I am talking about definite purposes. If you don't have any products yet, it's not too late. You can start now to begin to convert your time into products.

You may be wondering what I mean by products. When I say products I do not mean just clothes or phones or IPad. By-products, I mean added values. Products could be the values you added to yourself or to others. Products could be in the form of perfecting your gifts and talents. Products could be in the form of researching and experimenting in a particular field of medicine or engineering etc. and gaining more knowledge in that area of life. Products could be in the form of books you've read or teachings you listen to via audio or video. Products could be in the form of books you have written from the values you have added to yourself.

Products could be in the form of songs written and albums produced. Products could be in the form of scientific discoveries you have made. Products could people, disciples and teams you've built. Whatever system of self-improvement you practice to make you are a better person could be regarded as the avenues with which you could produce products. Products could also be in the form of an improved character and virtue. There is no ending to the list of things we could call products. It is important that any value you add to yourself should be converted to tangible products that could benefit humanity. These products could also be in the form of disciples or mentees you have impacted. They could also be in the form of people you are coaching or improving on a daily or weekly basis.

What you must know is that all of these products are only possible thanks to the amount of time you are able to invest and convert. You must learn to produce products if you desire to be great. It doesn't matter if you haven't produced any product before. You can start gradually like I did with just one product a year and then graduate from one product to two products and so on. I assure you if you do that your story will be like mine.

My story had a happy ending and the happy ending that I had was that I got to a point when I began to realize that I was producing four products a year; that is one product per quarter. It made things easier for me. It just made me know that I decide my discipline; how much I am able to discipline myself, to cut off all unwanted things and how much I am able to cut off all distractions. It showed me how much I am able to cut off all trivialities and frivolities around me. It thought me how much I am able to put my friends down because I use to be a people guy. I used to just spend time with everybody, trying to make everybody happy and that was what took a lot of my life. You see, it is better to purposefully spend time with people talking about things that could improve them or talk about things that could improve me than to just waste time discussing irrelevant things.

We could also be talking about things that could improve our world, improve and build each one of us. When we spend time discussing like this, we are purposefully adding value to each other and purposefully sharpening ourselves. We are purposely spending the time to better ourselves. But in those days I used to just spend time with people just to spend time and try to make everybody happy and not to make people think badly about me. And I saw that there were no products, there were no results to show for my life.

> "In your life, there are going to be constant
> demands for your time and attention.
> How are you going to decide which of those
> demands gets resources? The trap many
> people fall into is to allocate their time to
> whoever screams loudest, and their talent
> to whatever offers them the fastest reward.
> That's a dangerous way to build a strategy."
> CLAYTON M. CHRISTENSEN

Our world is structured in such a way that you will be ignorant and unaware of the fact that your life is disappearing gradually and that you are left only with very little life and time. There are so many things and people craving your attention such that you could so easily forget that you have a purpose to fulfill within a specified time on the earth. Society has got a lot of activities and attractions to steal your time and to make you think less about your diminishing life. Don't be deceived! Your life is diminishing. Time keeps passing by the day. It's a pity that you are not being told this truth even in your churches and schools. Nobody is telling you this reality. I want you to know that you have what it takes to convert your diminishing life into products. Not just one product a year but multiple products.

Can you imagine if I just continued measuring my life just by one product a year, and let's say I started by 25years of age, that means in the next 25years I will only have twenty-five products? Can you imagine if I just measured my life by one product a year when I could have produced one product a day? It's a pity that majority of people on earth are either not measuring their lives at all or are measuring their lives by just one product a year. How could you waste a whole three hundred and sixty-five days producing only one product when you could intentionally produce at least one product every day? If you are determined and hardworking, producing one product every day will become an easy thing to do. If you think it's not possible, let me explain it to you as I continue my story.

So later on my story continued and I said I am going to turn my life into producing a product a month. I must have a product, a visible product in a month. Either they are going to be products of saved people, or they are going to be products of leaders raised, or products of churches built or they are going to be products of organizations started or they are going to be in form of problems resolved or products of books written or books read or in the form of my growth level, my understanding level, my connection and my relationship level with God. There must be different things that you want to measure your results with. Once I resolved to produce one product a month, I started managing my time more strictly, making sure that none of it was wasted on irrelevant things.

> *"Time is the only commodity in life that*
> *cannot be bought, sold, borrowed, given*
> *out as a gift and it cannot be inherited.*
> *"Time is the scarcest resource and unless it*
> *is managed nothing else can be managed."*
> PETER F. DRUCKER

I didn't just resolve to produce one product a month, I disciplined myself to make sure it happened just as I planned it. I continued learning more and adding more value to myself. God helped me and just by seeking and searching and by working on myself and by training myself and by disciplining myself, I got to a point when I started producing one product per day. I mean, no day passes without producing a product. I began to take an inventory of my life per day. I was conscious of my time every day and made sure no minute of it was wasted but that all of it was converted into some products in my life and in the lives of others.

Take an inventory of your life. Begin to live an intentional life. Draw out some goals and targets of what you want to do in life, what you want to contribute to the world. You should have something even if very little, that you want to convert your life to producing. Maybe you need to start by a yearly assessment. But your life must be planned in such a way that you could get to a stage when you can say every day of your life is being converted to a product. You see, I started out by saying every year of my life was being converted to a product and that was a huge success for me. It was a big joy for me. Then I went to a place of converting my year into two products and then to converting my year into three products and then into four products. Now I produce products per hour. I add value to multitudes of people all over the world hourly.

Do you want to convert your time into products monthly or daily? Then your lifestyle must change. You must choose what you do with your time. You must not just do things because everybody is doing them. You must stop living under the pressure of the environment and surrounding and culture and tradition. You don't even have to attend all the numerous church services every day that does not add value to your life. Invest your time into activities that add value to your life and not just doing things because you are religious. Your Christian life is supposed to be about your personal relationship with God. It is supposed to be about you and God alone. Not you and church or an organization or some religious gatherings. Your life is about you and your God alone.

Don't live your life not knowing what to do with your time. If you don't have any results to show for all your passing time, then you must have been trivializing time and you must have been living your life carelessly.

Take charge of your life and multiply it. Be in control of your life and your time. Stop doing things as if you are a robot. Stop living as if you are been controlled and manipulated by other forces outside of you. Start living a life with God. Start having unity and intimacy with God. Find out his mind, his will and his purpose for you. Discover what you could do with your life and empower yourself in that area. Add value to yourself in that your area of calling. Get all the knowledge and wisdom needed to produce products per day or per month of your life. Begin to think of how you could maximize the time you have through hard work and through concentration. Start searching and researching about how to develop your skills and talents. Apply all that you have learned and then begin to produce something valuable through your skills, through your profession, and through your knowledge. Make sure that you intentionally bring out results and positive products and the world will celebrate you.

WHAT SHOULD I DO WITH MY VACATION? CONVERT YOUR VACATION INTO PRODUCTS

The proof that most people don't know how to measure their life by converting time into products is reflected in what they do with their free vacation time. I don't understand how people could have vacation and just be playing around especially white Europeans. White people during their vacation, just go and lie down under the sun and say they are tanning. They just lie down for two hours, three hours in the sun. Four hours is gone and they are still lying down until eventually the whole day passes and all they did was to lie down under the sun. They lie down for one week, two weeks and even a month. The problem is not with the lying down. But how can you go and lie down your life? What a waste of life!

That is a vacation! It is the best time for you to be productive because you are not being distracted by work. You are not spending your life away or selling it out in work or for a job. You have all the time to yourself now and under your control. There is no boss to control your time for you. There is no school timetable to dictate how you should use your time and the power is yours to do with your time whatever you want. Is it not the best time for you to invest your life and your time into producing some products of greatness? Is this not the time for you to convert that time into some added value to yourself? Instead of you to make the best out of that time, you are just pouring it out for nothing. You are just wasting your life sleeping or lying down under the sun. You are a life waster.

Another group of people who waste their vacations is university students. The majority of students schooling in Ukraine, for example, spend their holiday just sleeping, eating and watching movies. After watching as many movies as they want and sleep away their life, the next thing that sets in is boredom. You begin to hear them complaining "Oh! This holiday is so boring" I am tired of staying at home. Can you imagine that! Why are they complaining of boredom? Because they don't know what else to do with their precious time. They do not understand that they are holding the greatest wealth in the world under their control and hence do not know what to do with it. To not know what to do during the vacations is just a proof that society and the school system has stolen your life from you. You can no longer do anything meaningful with your life if there is no school time table to tell you when to wake up, when to study and when to be in class. It's a pity that your life is no longer in your hands but in the hands of your school management. When school vacates, your life vacates alongside. What a tragedy! What a waste of life!

Vacation time is the best time to do solitude because you could just take two weeks of it or one week of it and just isolate yourself. And when you isolate yourself, you can just begin to convert that time of vacation into any product you want. If you want to do an invention, for example, you go and do the research, go and put the research materials together and you use that vacation time to study it and do the experiments and you convert that time into the products that you want.

At other times you might have another mission. Let's say you have a mission of writing books. So you could use your vacation time to go into solitude and before you come out you have written a whole book. For example, I never go on vacation without coming out with two or three books written but only thanks to my solitude.

Let's look at the story of three students who were in their second year of medical school in Ukraine. **Joseph** who was from Nigeria, **Ashraf** who was from Jordan and **Sahil** from India. These three students were friends and classmates in the same medical university in Ukraine. During their second semester holiday which lasted from mid-June to 1st September of that year, each of the students decided to spend that holiday doing different things with their lives.

Joseph who knew that he was called to becoming a pastor after medical school, decided to invest his time into his calling. He made up his mind to use that summer holiday to write an inspirational Christian book. He had to isolate himself for that three months in his room listening to Christian tapes, searching the scriptures online and researching the topic for which he has chosen to title his book after. He made sure he converted ten hours every day studying and adding value to himself in his area of calling. He did that for three months and by the time school was resuming he had written three books instead of just one that he intended to write. He became an author of three Christian literature just during one summer vacation.

Ashraf, on the other hand, decided to use his summer time for tourism, sleeping and watching movies. He traveled to the city of Odessa in Ukraine to see the sea port and the beautiful places there. He had fun, took photographs and posted on Facebook and Instagram for his friends to see how he was enjoying life. He spent one week in Odessa and returned back to his city. On getting back to his city, he spent two weeks at home just sleeping, eating and watching movies and that was his routine alongside chatting with friends on Facebook and all other social media. After two weeks he realized that he was bored and got tired of that cycle of sleeping, eating and watching movies. Luckily for him, a friend of his who was also from his country invited him for a summer trip to a place called Bukovel, a ski resort in the western part of Ukraine. He hastily accepted the invitation without giving it a second thought as he saw it as a way to overcome his boredom. He felt since he didn't know what else to do with his precious vacation time, going for such a trip wouldn't be a bad idea. Two days after the invitation, they set out for the journey to Bukovel and spent a week there. Of course, it was another series of fun and picture taking. The rest of the vacation was used for nothing meaningful other than visiting friends, sleeping, watching movies, going for birthday parties and chatting on social media.

The third guy Sahil thought that the vacation time could be used to gain more clinical knowledge in the field of medicine and so decided to travel home to India for clinical practice. He was able to get acceptance from a private hospital in Delhi where he spent two months of his summer vacation. He was going to the hospital every day for two months and learning the clinical aspect of medicine. He was posted to the different departments of the hospital including radiology department, surgery department, nephrology department and endocrinology department. He learned so much about the clinical aspect of medicine as he was allowed to watch a few operations and actually see the practicality of what he had been taught in class before. What Sahil did was that he invested his time into gaining more knowledge in the field of medicine. He converted his vacation time into added value to himself.

Now, which of these three friends do you think understood the value of time? Which of them do you think will become great tomorrow if they repeated this same event for the next four years of their career?

Off course Sahil would become a better doctor tomorrow haven added so much value to himself in the field of medicine but only thanks to the power of time conversion.

Joseph, on the other hand, would also become a very enlightened and impactful pastor. He would no doubt be a renowned figure in society because he converted his time into added value to himself and into producing products in the form of Christian books.

Ashraf, however, will become a very bad doctor if he decides to practice medicine. He has not added value to himself but wasted his time in the frivolities of life. He is definitely a time waster and the possibility that he will ever become great tomorrow is very doubtful. He will most likely end up living the life of a mediocre. You see, life is predictable. What you do with your time now will dictate how your life will become tomorrow.

So to answer the question "What should I do with my vacation?" I would like to emphasize that vacation time is the greatest time. Convert that time into products. Every day of your life, every minute of your life should be converted into some products. Can you look back at your past vacations? Can you remember what you did with them? Do you have any products to show for them? It's a pity that all you have to show for your vacations are the parks you visited and the hotels you slept in. I feel sad for you that it is just the shopping you did and the beach or swimming pool you visited that come to your mind. All you could possibly remember to have done with your vacation time was all vanity and frivolities. Do you see now that you have been wasteful just like Ashraf? Has it not dawned on you that you didn't convert all your past vacations into products? Oh! What a waste! What a waste of precious time! What a waste of precious life!

As I round off this chapter, I want to remind you that you can start now to begin to measure your life by the products you produce per day. Begin to set daily goals for yourself and try to achieve them. Do not waste your vacation time, it is your most precious time. Invest your time and add value to your life because that is the only way to greatness.

In the next chapter, I am going to be revealing to you the true nature of time and how you can best utilize that to your advantage. I implore you to read on dear friends.

TIME PRINCIPLES
FROM CHAPTER THREE

1. Our world is structured in such a way for you not to even know and for you not to even be told and for you not to even think about it that your life is disappearing gradually and that you are left only with very little life and time.

2. Society has got a lot of activities and attractions to steal your time and to make you think less about your diminishing life. Don't be deceived!

3. The proof that most people don't know how to measure their life by converting time into products is reflected in what they do with their free vacation time.

4. That is a vacation! It is the best time for you to be productive because you are not being distracted by work.

5. To not know what to do during the vacations is just a proof that society and the school system has stolen your life from you.

6. When school vacates, your life vacates alongside. What a tragedy! What a waste of life!

7. Vacation time is the best time to do solitude because you could just take two weeks of it or one week of it and just isolate yourself. And when you

isolate yourself, you can just begin to convert that time of vacation into any product you want.

8. Let's say you have a mission of writing books. So you could use your vacation time to go into solitude and before you come out you have written a whole book.

9. You see life is predictable. What you do with your time now will dictate how your life will become tomorrow.

10. So to answer the question "What should I do with my vacation?" I would like to emphasize that vacation time is the greatest time. Convert that time into products. Every day of your life, every minute of your life should be converted into some products.

HOW TO BECOME GREAT
THROUGH TIME CONVERSION

1. Discover what you could do with your life
   and empower yourself in that area. Add value
   to yourself in that your area of calling.

2. Get all the knowledge and wisdom needed to
   produce products per day or per month of your life.

3. Begin to think of how you could maximize
   the time you have through hard work
   and through concentration.

4. Start searching and researching about how
   to develop your skills and talents.

5. Apply all that you have learned and then
   begin to produce something valuable
   through your skills, through your profession,
   and through your knowledge.

6. Make sure that you intentionally bring
   out results and positive products and
   the world will celebrate you.

7. If you want to do an invention, for example,
   you go and do the research, go and put the
   research materials together and then use
   your vacation time to study it and do the
   experiments and you would have converted
   that time into the products that you want.

8. Don't live your life not knowing what to do with your time. If you don't have any results to show for all your passing time, then you must have been trivializing time and you must have been living your life carelessly.

9. Take charge of your life and multiply it. Be in control of your life and your time!

10. Your life must be planned in such a way that you could get to a stage when you can say every day of your life is being converted to a product.

CHAPTER 4

THE MELTING CLOCKS

THE SALVADOR DALI STORY

Salvador Dali is among the most versatile and prolific artists of the twentieth century. He is perhaps best known for his 1931 painting *The Persistence of Memory*, showing *melting clocks* in a landscape setting.

Salvador Dalí was born on May 11, 1904, in Figueres, Spain. At an early age, Salvador was producing highly sophisticated drawings, and both of his parents strongly supported his artistic talent. It was here that his parents built him an art studio before he entered art school. Upon recognizing his immense talent, Salvador Dalí's parents sent him to drawing school in Spain, in 1916.

One of Dalí's most famous paintings produced in his lifetime — and perhaps the best-known Surrealist work — was *The Persistence of Memory* (1931). The painting, sometimes called *Soft Watches*, shows melting pocket watches in a landscape setting.

There are different speculations as to what the melting clocks in Salvador Dali's paintings could mean. Some said it could refer to Dali's own memory of his childhood surroundings. Others suggest that the clock also symbolizes the decaying and therefore impermanent nature of our arbitrary way of keeping time.

While we cannot know for certain the true meaning, interpretation or analysis that Dali himself intended for his painting, I will, however, want to explain two of the assumptions about the meaning of the melting clocks that are most striking and most relevant to the subject matter of this book.

The first assumption; It is said that the painting conveys several ideas within the image, chiefly that time is not rigid and everything is destructible. I want you to pay attention to this line "Time is not rigid" It is destructible. It melts away before you know it. This is exactly what I have been trying to get across to you from the beginning of this book. The idea that time melts and vanishes whether we like it or not is what the melting clocks of Salvador Dali depict. I have said before that as time diminishes, life diminishes alongside. In agreement with the first assumption of the melting clocks, I want to state at this point that nothing is stable in life including life itself. Everything diminishes and everything is destructible. Since everything is destructible including life, you should, therefore, make the best out of life while it lasts. The only way to get the best out of the diminishing life is to invest it into the fulfillment of your purpose. To invest your life, you must invest your time and make sure it doesn't just melt away like Salvador Dali's melting clock. The thought that your time and your life will melt away should create a sense of urgency to do something of worth with it before it all melts away. If you are given twenty-four hours of your life every day to do something with it, what would you do with it before it melts in the evening? Sadly so many people stand and watch their life melt away every day without taking advantage of it to produce something of worth. This refusal to convert this melting life into a product happens repeatedly for fifty, sixty or maybe seventy years of a man's life after which he dies with nothing left to benefit the next generation. What a waste of precious life! A life that could have been used to positively impact humanity is allowed to melt away into vanity. The tragedy of life is that it comes just once and before you know it, it is gone. Since life comes just once, I encourage you to give it your best shot. I dare you to maximize your life. You can create the best out of your life by understanding the wealth of time and converting that time into the life that you were created to live. I mean to say convert your time into fulfilling your purpose. I will be emphatic about this; the best way to convert your time into products is through the power of isolation. It is easier to convert your time into products when you move away from any distractions. Do not watch your life melt away just like that for life is too precious to waste it doing nothing.

The second assumption; others believe that the melting and distorted clocks symbolize the erratic passage of time that we experience while dreaming.

I find the second assumption of the melting clocks fascinating because it depicts the actual state of a majority of people on the earth. The tragedy of our age is that a greater percentage of people living today are only living in the dream world. Have you ever woken up from a dream and expected it to still be the middle of the night and are surprised to find that it is already morning? That is the realm in which most people live their lives; the realm of dreams. Everyone dreams of greatness and expects it to happen in the future automatically. The problem with dreams is that they are always futuristic and gives a deceptive impression that there is still enough time to actualize them. The tragedy, however, is that you soon realize that the time you thought you had to fulfill the dreams had melted away before your very eyes. You suddenly come to terms with the reality that you are now sixty or seventy years old but did none of the things you dreamt you were going to do.

> *"Habitual procrastinators will readily testify to all the lost opportunities, missed deadlines, failed relationships and even monetary losses incurred just because of one nasty habit of putting things off until it is often too late."*
> STEPHEN RICHARDS,

The only thing you can do with the dreams when you realize it's already morning is to regret wasting your life while you had all the time. You only regret not converting time into fulfilling your dreams while you had the time. That is not the kind of life you should live.

Dear friends I do not want you to live in the dream world because time erratically passes away in that world. Come to reality and begin to act now. Actualize the dreams now and don't procrastinate them for the future. Use every second, minute and hour that you have to fulfill your life's calling, your purpose, and your dreams. Convert every passing time of your life before it melts away. Greatness is never achieved in the realm of dreams but in the realm of reality and the only way to achieving that greatness is to convert your time into added value to yourself and then to others. Your dream will only benefit humanity when you make it tangible by living it out. You are only great to the degree you impacted others with your life. Take hold of your passing time and convert it into living your dreams. Only then can you truly fulfill the great destiny that you were called to fulfill.

"Dare to live the life you have dreamed for yourself. Go forward and make your dreams come true."
RALPH WALDO EMERSON

SALVADOR DALI CONVERTED HIS TIME

He didn't just paint melting clocks, he understood what he painted. Salvador Dali understood the value of time and hence invested his time into developing and perfecting his painting gifts. He constantly refined his talents by going into solitude to learn and rehearse the art of painting. His works were so exceptional that people paid a fortune just to get his drawings. His artwork and influence can be seen everywhere around the world. He is one of the greatest Spanish painters of all times. He had a brilliant technical mastery of the art of painting thanks to his time conversion. He invested time into gaining mastery in the art of painting and that made him one of the most refined and accomplished painters of the 20th century.

Salvador Dali made painting his lifestyle making sure that none of his time was wasted doing something else. No wonder he had a lot of first class artworks. He was so creative that all his works reflected that creativity. The reason for such a high level of creativity was that he constantly separated himself from distractions. You must understand that your creativity comes alive when you spend time alone focusing on your projects without distractions. Most of his paintings were gotten in the place of isolation and they came to him in the form of dreams and imaginations. However, because he understood the value of the time, he invested his time into converting all of those dreams and imaginations into tangible products.

Concerning one of his paintings in 1951 "Christ of Saint John of the Cross" Dali wrote: "In the first place in 1950, I had a cosmic dream in which I saw this image in color and which in my dream represented the nucleus of the atom. This nucleus later took on a metaphysical sense; I considered it the very unity of the universe, the Christ!

Salvador Dali did not only have the dream but he converted the dream into visible products within one year. He finished the painting at the end of autumn in 1951 and sent it to London for the exhibition. Dear friends, you can turn all your imaginations and dreams into tangible products if only you will invest your time into working hard to achieve that.

From the same dream, he got an inspiration to paint another work "The Ascension of Christ ". This is a proof that you can produce as many products as you want in life if you just apply the principle of time conversion. Salvador Dali gave birth to so many products in his lifetime but only thanks to the power of time conversion.

YOUR LIFE EVAPORATES. WHAT WILL YOU DO WITH IT?

Man is like a breath, his days are like a passing shadow. Your life on earth is but for a few days and before you know it you are no more. Your life is like a mist that appears for a little time and then vanishes. Your time on earth soon comes to an end before you know it. It evaporates like water and it's no more. Since your life evaporates quickly, it is wisdom to learn how to number your days. Not just to number your days but to make each passing day productive. You have just one life here on earth and it behooves you to make the best out of it. Give that your one life your best input so that it could yield the best output in the form of products that will impact your world positively. What are you going to do with this your evaporating life, will you allow it varnish into vanity or you want to reproduce it? To allow your life varnish into vanity without reproducing it would mean to live a wasted life.

To reproduce your life is to convert it into tangible products for the benefit of humanity. To reproduce your life is to impact the world with it. Many people, however, have left this earth without leaving their mark in the sand of time. Their lives evaporated into vanity without impacting the world with it. You don't want to join the queue of life wasters. You don't want to be numbered among those who wasted their time here on earth. You, therefore, must learn to make the best of the time you have now by converting it into some added values and products. You were born for more than just living in mediocrity and dying after your time here evaporates. You were born to convert the evaporating life into some impact on humanity. You are to use this one life to make a difference in your world. You are to invest your time and not waste it.

Remember, every day is a gift from God and within that gift is twenty-four hours given freely to you. You are the one to decide what to do with that time. You are to convert that twenty-four hours into products and added value to yourself and for others. Do not allow it evaporate just like that without making the best out of it. To allow your time evaporate each day without a product to show for it is to allow your life evaporate into vanity.

> *"The bad news is time flies. The good news is you're the pilot."*
> Michael Altshuler

Look at your life now. You are not as young as you were when you were born. Some part of your life has evaporated. Sadly, you may have no tangible product to show for the evaporated part of your life. Perhaps the world has not benefited from your presence here on earth. No nation has been impacted by your life. Your past years may not have produced anything that could benefit the next generation. It's a pity that you perhaps wasted those years. It's a tragedy to find that your life is evaporating without a product to show for it.

LOOK AT THE FUTURE

Dear friends, it is true that you may have lost some time in the past. You may have allowed your life melt away with your time, but the good news is that you still have the future. Now, look at the next twenty or thirty years of your life. Project into the future. What are you going to do with this amount of time? What are you going to do with your nearest future? It is true that the next twenty or thirty years of your life will still evaporate soon, but the question is; will you allow it just evaporate like that? Don't you want to make some impact on your world? Don't you want to be numbered among the great men and women who changed the world for good? If your answer is yes, then you should begin to lay hold of every minute of your life and convert it into something of value to benefit the world. Never allow any of your time to be wasted on the frivolities of life. The future belongs to you. You decide what you want to do with it.

Invest your life into what you were born to do. Make every minute of your life count. Redeem every minute of your life and convert it into greatness. Convert your time into solutions for the problems of the world and your immediate neighborhood. You were given your life to make it a solution to the problems of the world but it is only through time conversion that you can create that solution that the world needs. If you leave this world without solving the problems for which you were born, then you are a failure. It doesn't matter how long you live on planet earth, if by the time your whole life has evaporated, you have not solved the problems you were created to solve; then you wasted your life. Do not waste time for that is equal to wasting life. Invest your evaporating life and reap greatness. Invest your evaporating time and leave a legacy behind for future generations. Take this short time that you have on earth and convert it into greatness. Do not live for emptiness. Do not waste your evaporating life pursuing the vanities of life. One thing is needful and that is converting your time into fulfilling your purpose on the earth. You have just one life here on earth. Do not waste it.

Dear friends, I do hope this chapter was an eye-opener for you. Now that you have seen the true nature of your life and your time, you should try as much as possible to lay hold of your diminishing life and convert it into some products for humanity like Salvador Dali did. Stop the procrastination and start acting now.

In the next chapter, I will be revealing to you that we are in a race and my desire is to show you how to win the race. Please follow me as we move to the next chapter and you will be surprised how easy it is to win in the race of life. See You!

LIFE PRINCIPLES FROM
CHAPTER FOUR

1. "Time is not rigid" It is destructible. It melts away before you know it.

2. The only way to get the best out of the diminishing life is to invest it into the fulfillment of your purpose.

3. The thought that your time and your life will melt away should create a sense of urgency to do something of worth with it before it all melts away.

4. This refusal to convert this melting life into a product happens repeatedly for fifty, sixty or maybe seventy years of a man's life after which he dies with nothing left to benefit the next generation. What a waste of precious life!

5. The tragedy of life is that it comes just once and before you know it, it is gone. Since life comes just once, I encourage you to give it your best shot.

6. Do not watch your life melt away just like that for life is too precious to waste it doing nothing.

7. The problem with dreams is that they are always futuristic and gives a deceptive impression that there is still enough time to actualize them. The tragedy, however, is that you soon realize that the time you thought you had to fulfill the dreams had melted away before your very eyes.

8. Come to reality and begin to act now. Actualize the dreams now and don't procrastinate them for the future. Use every second, minute and hour that you have to fulfill life's calling, your purpose, and your dreams.

9. Your dream will only benefit humanity when you make it tangible by living it out.

10. Take hold of your passing time and convert it into living your dreams. Only then can you truly fulfill the great destiny that you were called to fulfill?

HOW TO BECOME GREAT
THROUGH TIME CONVERSION

1. It is easier to convert your time into products when you move away from any distractions.

2. You can turn all your imaginations and dreams into tangible products if only you will invest your time into working hard to achieve that.

3. You can produce as many products as you want in life if you just apply the principle of time conversion.

4. Since your life evaporates quickly, it is wisdom to learn how to number your days. Not just to number your days but to make each passing day productive.

5. To reproduce your life is to convert it into tangible products for the benefit of humanity. To reproduce your life is to impact the world with it.

6. You were born for more than just living in mediocrity and dying after your time here evaporates. You were born to convert the evaporating life into some impact on humanity.

7. Begin to lay hold of every minute of your life and convert it into something of value to benefit the world. Never allow any of your time to be wasted on the frivolities of life.

8. Invest your life into what you were born to do. Make every minute of your life count. Redeem every minute of your life and convert it into greatness.

9. You were given your life to make it a solution to the problems of the world but it is only through time conversion that you can create that solution that the world needs.

10. Invest your evaporating life and reap greatness. Invest your evaporating time and leave a legacy behind for future generations. Take this short time that you have on earth and convert it into greatness.

CHAPTER 5

THE RACE OF LIFE

My congratulations to you dear friends for reading thus far. In this chapter, I am going to be proving to you that every one of us is in a race and we have a limited time to finish that race. How well you run determines whether or not you will win or lose. But my agenda here is to teach you to win using the lives of Charles Darwin and Ludwig Van Beethoven as illustrations. I encourage you to read on till the end and don't forget to pay attention to the principles I will be sharing with you within the pages of this chapter

RACING AGAINST TIME

We are in a race, my dear. Life is a race. You are racing against time. Your life is such that you are running a race against a diminishing life. Whether you like it or not your life is passing away. Even if you don't do anything, your life is still reducing, and it keeps diminishing. Your life is disappearing. Whether you are aware of it or not, your life is still disappearing. It's pouring out; it keeps diminishing. So the race we are in is a race against the disappearing life. Instead of your life just disappearing or being wasted or spent, you are racing to make sure that it is being converted, making sure that it is being actually invested. In this race of life, you want to make sure that every minute that is passing, every second that is passing is being converted and been invested. That is the race you are in. You are in a race against time. You are in a race against seconds. You are in a race against minutes and you are in a race against every hour not being lost. You are in a race of fight, you are fighting that no hour is lost, that every hour is invested, either in value added to yourself or in value added to others or in products that you are producing that must change the world or promote the kingdom of God. You are racing to create physical products that you could show and that are tangible. Products that you intend to benefit other people and the world at large with.

So you are in a race against your diminishing life, your diminishing seconds, your diminishing minute and your disappearing hours. You must fight to make sure that your life does not just disappear into thin air. It is a battle of not allowing those your seconds, those your minutes to just disappear into thin air. Do not allow your life to just fly out of your own hands. Do not allow your life to just disappear into some abstract mirage. You are in a race of converting it into value provided for yourself, into value provided to others and into a product. You are in a race against your disappearing life. And the thing is that the race must be yielding if you win. You win when you are able to convert all your disappearing time or the disappearing life into products. You win when you are able to convert that time into an investment, into seeds or fruits or products of cultivating your own land or products in other people's lives. When you are able to create values in yourself or in others then you have won the race. When you succeed in showing the real products that this disappearing life has produced, then you are said to be a winner; then you could be called a great man but only thanks to the power of conversion.

The good thing about winning the race against time is that even though your time is diminishing you always have a product to show for it. When your race on earth is finally over and your time has completely disappeared, what will continue to live on in the lives of others are the products you were able to produce from your invested time. When great men die in the race of life, they continue to live because the world can still benefit from their products. The world still uses the materials produced by men who maximally invested their time to produce products while they were alive. Even though most of them are dead, yet their impact lives on. The world still enjoys their discoveries and inventions. In fact most of the great men who converted their time to products although late are still making more impact in the world today than a greater percentage of people who are still alive. The likes of Thomas Edison and Nikola Tesla are dead but they are still touching the world with their inventions and discoveries and believe me, generations to come will still be enjoying their impact. How did they come about their inventions and discoveries? They simply invested their time and made sure their time didn't just diminish into thin air. They knew they were in a race against time and intentionally fought so hard to win the race. The products they invented are the proofs that they won the race of life. Today they live on in their products and still impact the world through their products. It is a pity that dead men are still impacting the world while men who are still alive are wasting away, roaming the world without an understanding of what to do with their time.

Most people end their race here on earth with no products to show for all their time they spent on earth. The majority of people who have passed on left nothing of value to the next generation and this is simply because they failed to convert their time into products and added value to themselves and to others. The few who did convert their time into products left something behind for the next generation and today they are celebrated as great men and heroes. You must fight to invest your time into producing products and added value to your generation. You must not allow any of your time to pass by without adding value to yourself and reproducing your life in others. You will need an evidence to show the world that you didn't waste your time here on earth. Generations to come should benefit from the products of your time converted. I want to leave you with these questions; what products will you leave behind for future generations? When your life has completely disappeared, what products will you have to show for it? What evidence will you have to convince the next generation that you didn't waste your time while alive?

CHARLES DARWIN: A MAN WHO UNDERSTOOD THE VALUE OF TIME.

Charles Darwin is a very popular name in the world. It doesn't matter your country of origin, you must have heard of his name if you ever studied biology in school. He is probably the greatest scientist the world has known so far. He is considered the most famous and most influential scientist of the 19th century. He had very revolutionary ideas that illuminated the scientific world. According to Julian Huxley, Darwin's idea "is the most powerful and most comprehensive idea that has ever arisen on earth. He published the theory of evolution and wrote a book on the origin of species. However, my intention here is not to talk about the theory of evolution but to talk about how he invested his time. Even though he was an unbeliever, he did what Christians should be doing. He understood the power of time conversion and used his time for research and experiments. Whether you like it or not, you cannot erase his name from the pages of history nor from textbooks of medical biology.

Therefore, looking away from his evolution theory, one striking thing about this great geologist was that he understood the value of time. He knew that time is life and that wasting time is equal to wasting life. His understanding of time was reflected in the quote below.

> *"A man who dares to waste one hour of time has not discovered the value of life."*
> CHARLES DARWIN

In this quote, he advised people to invest their time instead of wasting it. He argued that to waste one hour is a proof of lack of understanding of life. He stated that when you waste one hour of your time you have wasted your life. In other words, Charles Darwin understood that the value of life is in time. He understood that one hour could make a whole lot of difference in the life of a man. A lot could be achieved in one hour if properly invested. Have you ever wasted an hour? If your answer is yes, then Charles Darwin is saying that you do not understand the value of life.

If you knew that time is life, would you still waste time? If you understood that to possess time is to possess life would you still trivialize time? Everyone on earth is afraid of losing his/her life, and only a few are afraid of losing their time. If you knew that your time is your life you would protect it as much as you protect your life. However, ignorance of this fact is the number one reason why you have wasted your time and allowed it fly away unprotected. One of the most painful realizations in life is to all of a sudden discover that you had possessed things all along that you never knew you had. It is almost an unbearable pain to suddenly recognize the value of what you had been ignorant of, which had been in your possession. To possess something and not know its value is torturous. To own something and not be aware of it could not only be annoying, but fatal too. That is why most people had all the time but did nothing with it. They died leaving behind no invention or product that they could be remembered for.

Charles Darwin invested most of his time experimenting and researching the origin of life. He intensively studied and used his time working so hard to publish his book on transmutation. Today you will not graduate from a secondary school without learning about Charles Darwin. Though he is dead but he lives on in the minds of so many people today; both students and teachers alike. Though he is dead, he still speaks through the pages of his books and via his theories on evolution but only thanks to his understanding of the value of time.

The greatest treasure in life is the possession of time. Tragically, though, it is that same time that is often least treasured or valued by men who still possess it. Dead men have lost possession of this treasure but those who have it do not treasure it. All men have been given time, but only a few men know its value. To have something does not mean to understand it. Most people who possess life, in reality, do not quite understand that they possess life only because they possess time. That is a fundamental tragedy about life. Those who possess time are often not aware of its value.

If you understand the value of time, you will convert it into products. The reason I am able to produce five books a month is because I understand the value of time. So I am multiplying myself in five different products every month and I have gotten to a place whereby to produce a product in a month is no more a target. Because in a month I influence so many people, I produce products and results now not on monthly basis, not even on daily basis. I produce results hourly. For example, one hour of time every morning and one hour in the evening I am adding value to people all over the world through my Facebook live broadcast. I also make sure that three hours every day, I add value to myself by listening to messages and by doing self-education. If I have time I spend up to six hours a day producing products in myself because that is what makes me valuable. That is like going to my laboratory where I do research and make myself better. By researching and making myself better, I produce better results. Besides, I have books I am writing and people I am teaching how to write books and how to become better pastors. You also can become a better person and produce better products if you will just learn to invest your time properly. You can become great by multiplying yourself through time conversion into different products but that will only be possible if you understand the value of time.

A LIFE WITHOUT REGRETS

Life is so short. The day is so short. Even though we have twenty-four hours a day, and we sleep at least for eight hours, we cook, we eat, bath, brush our teeth, wear clothes and spend time with family members for like another five to six hours, and we will still have perhaps eight to ten hours left to ourselves. If you can take out three to four hours a day and invest it into producing a product in a day that will be a very high caliber of productivity. If producing a product, in a day is difficult for your, maybe you can start with a year, producing one concrete product per year. Then graduate to having two products in a year and then to three products in a year and four products in a year. As you begin to grow and get better, you can then begin to produce one product each month. If you could live such a life of producing one product every month, then you will become one of the most effective human beings on earth. It means that you can decide the results that each one of your passing days could produce. When you can actually measure your day by how much time is converted into products, then you are a great force on the earth. When you can actually monitor your passing life and be in control and be in charge of your time and making sure that you are actually converting every passing day into something, then you will never regret it. That is how to live a life without regret.

If you don't monitor your life, you will regret it. If you don't measure your life you will regret it. If you don't convert your time into products you will regret it. If you don't multiply your life you will soon find out that your life is almost finished with nothing to show for it. If you don't make your time count now, you will regret it later. There are many people today in their 60's and 70's regretting how they wasted their lives and wishing that they invested it. They are wishing they could get their time back, but it's all gone. If you don't want to regret your life later, then begin to invest your time, begin to measure your life. Measure your life by the products and by the results you produce! Measure your life by the value you've added! Measure your life by how much of your time you converted! Every man must choose what they want to do with their time to avoid regret in the future. You have to choose what you want to do with your time. But if you desire to be great in life and live a life of no regret the number one thing you should do with time is to INVEST TIME.

HOW MUCH TIME ARE YOU WILLING TO INVEST?

Ludwig Van Beethoven lived for only 56 years. He was deaf but he was able to invest about fifty thousand hours into his musical calling and became one of the best musical composers in history. He invested his time into his own land of promise and that is why the whole world is talking about him.

Beethoven was born on 16th, December 1770 in Bonn of Germany. His father was a singer in a local palace choir.

Beethoven **couldn't afford to go to school because of his poor family background**. However, he had an extravagant love for music at a very tender age. He was potentially gifted in music. His father wanted to make use of his potential to make a big fortune. As a result, Beethoven had to practice playing clavicorn and violin day and night under his father's pressure.

It was this constant practice every day and night that made him exceptionally skillful. He constantly invested his time into learning and perfecting new skills. He didn't waste his time like other kids of his age but he disciplined himself under his father to learn and become the best in his area of gifting. He would overwork himself beyond his father's demands and often refuse to stop playing the piano when his father wanted to finish rehearsals for the day. He was so passionately in love with the chords he played that he wouldn't want the practice sessions to end.

Even though he was from a poor background, he didn't allow that deter him from converting his time wisely. Poverty is irrelevant when there is proper time conversion. You don't have to be rich to understand time conversion. Therefore no one can use poverty as an excuse for not becoming great. Beethoven despite his poor background invested his time into adding value to himself. He lived in isolation rehearsing and gaining mastery over his musical skills. He shrank from societal distractions and lived in isolation converting his time into refining and perfecting his skills.

Beethoven had a performance on a stage for the first time when he was only seven years old and he made a huge success. Some famous musicians considered him as the second Mozart. Beethoven learned how to compose music from Nifo and published his first work named Concerto in A minor when he was 11. He went to Vienna to learn how to compose music from Mozart and Haydn.

Instead of just going to a normal school, he was wise enough to focus on his talents. Even though they were from a poor background, he was able to invest so much of his time into learning the act of composing music. He invested his life into his purpose and became one of the best in the world. He became great thanks to the power of time conversion. He regularly practiced being alone converting his time into added value to himself and that is why he was able to give birth to great music. You must understand that all great things come through time conversion.

Beethoven received his first success in 1800. Nevertheless, he was troubled with a terrible matter for years at that time. He found that he has **become a deaf person**. There couldn't be anything more terrible than that for a musician.

Despite his hearing loss, he was still able to compose many more beautiful music including The Second Symphonies from 1803 onward. His music was exceptionally unique and warm to the heart.

In 1823, he finished his masterpiece named The Ninth Symphonies. By the time his ninth symphonies was performed that night in Vienna, he was profoundly deaf. Many years later his music is still as powerful, overwhelming and brilliant as ever. The most intriguing thing about his music is the fact that the composer of such beautiful music was unable to hear. He did not use the fact that he lost his hearing as an excuse to waste his life, rather he kept on investing his time and that earned him greatness.

His music impacted the world and transformed many lives. It changed the history of music. He is regarded as one of the giants of classical music and his influence on subsequent generations of composers was profound but this is only because he converted his time properly into added value to himself and to his generation.

BEETHOVEN UNDERSTOOD THE POWER OF CONVERSION

"It seemed unthinkable for me to leave the world forever before I had produced all that I felt called upon to produce"

Ludwig van Beethoven

From his quote above you could see that he was intentional about all the music he produced. He wasn't just giving birth to products, he understood that time was meant to be converted into products. He knew that which many people on earth do not know; that is the fact that life is only worth living if it is used to produce products for the good of humanity. Besides just converting time to products Beethoven also understood that every man has been called to produce a certain number of products within the time allocated to him to live on earth and that failure to hit the target would mean a wasted life. He understood his calling and soaked himself in it. He knew that the only way to live a life of no regret in this race of life is to invest and convert quality amount of time into producing products for the good of humanity.

What are you going to do with your life? Are you going to invest quality time into producing the number of products you were destined to produce for humanity or you are going to allow your time fly away without converting it into products? Do you want to lose in this race of life? How could you live your whole life without meeting up with the divine targets for your life? How could you waste your life just like that? Do you really want to live a life of no regret? Do you intend to leave a legacy for future generations? If your answer is yes then you may want to start following the example of Beethoven. You may want to start focusing on investing and converting your time into exploring your area of calling. It doesn't matter what your area of calling is, if you could invest quality time in it then you will be sure to produce the quality amount of products. The world awaits your products. Humanity lives in eager expectation of your products. Begin to convert your time into products. Begin to gain the mastery over your talents and gifting. Begin to invest quality time. Start the conversion process and birth your products. Convert every minute and hour of your life into perfecting your calling. Do not leave the world without producing as many products as you were destined to produce. Do not deprive the world the gift of your products. You too can become great but only thanks to the number of hours you are able to convert into products.

My congratulations to you once more for reading through this chapter. I believe that you have made up your mind to win in this race of life. I do hope you will begin to fight for your minutes and your seconds and not allow them to disappear without producing some products. If you could learn from Charles Darwin, then you will never waste an hour again. If you could learn from Beethoven, then you will produce as many products as you have been called upon to produce. Run well and win in this race of life by converting your time into added values and products.

I am about to show you a treasure in the next chapter. That treasure changed my life for good. Do you really want to be great? If yes, then let's proceed to discover that treasure. See you in the next chapter.

TIME PRINCIPLES
FROM CHAPTER FIVE

1. Life is a race. You are racing against time.
    Your life is such that you are running a race
    against a diminishing life. Whether you
    like it or not your life is passing away.

2. In this race of life, you want to make sure that
    every minute that is passing, every second that is
    passing is being converted and been invested.

3. You must fight to make sure that your life does
    not just disappear into thin air. It is a battle of
    not allowing those your seconds, those your
    minutes to just disappear into thin air.

4. When your race on earth is finally over and your
    time has completely disappeared, what will continue
    to live on in the lives of others are the products you
    were able to produce from your invested time.

5. When great men die in the race of life,
    they continue to live because the world
    can still benefit from their products.

6. Most of the great men who converted their
    time to products although late are still making
    more impact in the world today than a greater
    percentage of people who are still alive.

7. It is a pity that dead men are still impacting
    the world while men who are still alive are

wasting away, roaming the world without an
understanding of what to do with their time.

8. You will need an evidence to show the world
   that you didn't waste your time here on earth.
   Generations to come should benefit from
   the products of your time converted.

9. When you waste one hour of your
   time you have wasted your life.

10. If you knew that your time is your life you would
    protect it as much as you protect your life.

HOW TO BECOME GREAT
THROUGH TIME CONVERSION

1. To own something and not be aware of it could not only be annoying, but fatal too. That is why most people had all the time but did nothing with it. They died leaving behind no invention or product that they could be remembered for.

2. The greatest treasure in life is the possession of time. Tragically, though, it is that same time that is often least treasured or valued by men who still possess it.

3. If you don't monitor your life, you will regret it. If you don't measure your life you will regret it. If you don't convert your time into products you will regret it. If you don't multiply your life you will soon find out that your life is almost finished with nothing to show for it.

4. If you don't want to regret your life later, then begin to invest your time, begin to measure your life. Measure your life by the products and by the results you produce!

5. If you desire to be great in life and live a life of no regret, the number one thing you should do with time is to INVEST TIME.

6. Life is only worth living if it is used to produce products for the good of humanity.

7. Every man has been called to produce a certain number of products within the time allocated to him to live on earth and failure to hit the target would mean a wasted life.

8. The world awaits your products. Humanity lives in eager expectation of your products. Begin to convert your time into products. Begin to gain the mastery over your talents and gifting.

9. Begin to invest quality time. Start the conversion process and birth your products.

10. You too can become great but only thanks to the number of hours you are able to convert into products.

CHAPTER 6

THE TREASURE CALLED SOLITUDE

Having read about the need to invest your time by converting it into products and added value in the last few chapters, you are about to learn the most effective way to convert your time into products and added value in this chapter. I will be showing you the best way you could win the race against time. I want to show you how to stop selling your life for peanuts. Do endeavor to read on till the end.

The greatest wealth in the world is the wealth of time. There is nothing more precious than the wealth of time. If you could realize that everything is made out of time, then you can convert your free time into anything you want. If you know what the treasure of time is worth, if you know that time is a resource, then you will actually be able to convert your time into any product you want. You will be able to convert your time into anything you decide to produce. Time can be converted to anything. It is from that time that everything is made. One of the things you could do with your time is to convert it into a treasure, a greater treasure and that treasure is called solitude. Solitude is a greater treasure than money. Solitude is a greater treasure than wealth.

What is solitude? Solitude is a purposeful and intentional time when you put yourself away alone with time and with the properties you need to convert that time into the product that you want to produce. Solitude is a time when you go into a determined period of making the best of your time. Solitude is the machine through which time can be converted into products. You are in solitude to convert your time into products. You are in solitude with the sole aim of getting the best out of that time.

Solitude is the measure through which you could concentrate on using your time. It is through solitude that you can convert your time into something of value. Solitude is a way of overcoming distraction so that you can convert your time into something of worth.

When you are able to overcome distractions, then you will be able to do something more specific, something more precise and definite with the time that you have. Therefore the time of solitude is the greatest treasure you could ever think about. Solitude is a wonderful treasure the world is still yet to discover.

NO SOLITUDE! NO BIRTH!

Do you know that nothing could be given birth to without solitude? You can really never give birth to anything in this world without solitude. Everything precious comes out of solitude. In life, anything precious can only be birthed thanks to solitude. Let's look at children for example. How do we give birth to children? How do we bring children into existence? You see, children are simply a product of solitude. On a domestic front, the most precious entity in the world is human life. A careful examination of the process of conception of human life takes us to a place of solitude. A man and a woman have to get to a place of privacy and solitude for them to be able to conceive. The reason is because before you will be able to give birth to children, you must, first of all, find a place where a man and a woman could be isolated. Solitude means isolation. Therefore for you be able to give birth to a child, two people must be isolated together. And that is when intimacy happens. Real intimacy is a product of solitude. It is that intimacy that eventually gives birth to children. So pregnancy and children are as a result of solitude. Just the way a man and a woman comes together in solitude to produce a fruit, so also conception takes place when a man gets together with his creator in solitude. Solitude with God is a place for pregnancy.

Solitude is also a place to receive great ideas and creative ideas from God. The power of imagination is strongest in the place of solitude. When you are always with people in a noisy environment, you can hardly think and have meditations. In a world as noisy as ours, only those who can isolate themselves will be able to think better and meditate better and hence have a higher chance of receiving innovative ideas and concepts.

> *"My imagination functions much better when I don't have to speak to people."*
> PATRICIA HIGHSMITH

Almost all the past medical breakthroughs and scientific discoveries were born out of solitude. About all innovations in history were given birth to thanks to the power of solitude. So there is always fruit coming out of solitude. That is why solitude is a treasure. Solitude is a wonderful treasure.

There is no treasure like solitude. So what I am trying to say is that a time of solitude will always produce some fruits. A time of solitude will always produce some results. Why? The reason is because the time of solitude is actually an opportunity to make time work for you. It is an opportunity to actually convert your time into something tangible. Solitude time is a period when you actually turn your time into some treasure. It is an opportunity for you to convert time into some form of wealth.

Therefore one of the greatest discoveries you could actually discover in life is the treasure of solitude. All other discoveries are products of solitude. Therefore if you want to give birth to any discoveries or inventions, you must start practicing solitude. If you want to give birth to your own books you must practice solitude. If you want to give birth to your own songs or musical albums, you must practice solitude. If you ever desire to give birth to anything at all, then you cannot do without solitude.

LIFE IS ABOUT CONVERSION

Do you remember the first and general principle of time? What was it? The first and general principle of time is that TIME MUST BE CONVERTED INTO PRODUCTS! Pay attention to this; Life is about CONVERSION. Life is all about conversion. Conversion of what? Conversion of time. Everything comes out of time. It is your ability to take your time and convert it into something that will decide if you are going to have a product or not. Do you have any products? Can you boast of any product you have given to the world to benefit humanity? The reason why you perhaps do not have products is simply because you are not converting your time into products. It is because you have neglected the greatest treasure in the world; the treasure of solitude.

Let me prove to you that life is all about conversion of time. Like a said before, everything comes out of time. For example, I am sure you do go to work. Let's assume you spend two hours on a bus going to and from work. While you were on that bus you were just looking around, looking at people and what they were wearing. You were having all kind of thoughts in your mind or just looking at the streets, looking at the weather, looking at trees and buildings. So one-hour passes and you were just looking around and nothing happens. Then when coming back also, you did the same thing; just looking at people and things like you did before. Do you know what you have done? You just wasted two precious hours doing nothing productive. Do you know what you just did? You just wasted life. You just wasted two hours of your life. Two hours of your life has just been thrown away.

Within that same two hours, let's also assume another person was sitting on that same bus with you but with a book. And he reads one hour when he is going to work and reads another one hour when returning home. What has he done? He just converted two hours into a product of added value and improved knowledge about whatever subject the book was about. It is like nothing has happened right? Just going to work right? Two people going to and returning from work; one just looking around and the other converting that same period of time, two hours into adding value to himself.

Within that two hours that has passed, he has finished reading a book. In two hours, he has just added weight, value to himself. Even though he was on the bus, he was able to isolate himself and used isolation to convert that time into a treasure. The time that could have been wasted. The time that could have just passed. He was able to convert that time into added value to himself.

Yet another person, traveling in the same bus is typing with his laptop. He is not even looking around, he is not seeing anybody. In one hour he has written one chapter of a book and in another one hour, he has written an extra one chapter. So just by going to and from work, he has written two chapters of a book. Imagine if he does that for a week, he would have written a whole book containing at least ten chapters. If he does that for a month, he could write three or four books just by going to and returning from work. So what has happened? You would say "There was no time. We were all traveling. Just busy traveling. What was I supposed to do?" But that same time did not wait for you because you were traveling. The time kept counting and your life kept diminishing.

It is either you are converting time into a product or into a value chain or you are killing, wasting and throwing away your life. You must remember that whether you like it or not, every day your life is diminishing, your life is reducing and your life is pouring out. Whether you convert that diminishing life into something or you don't convert it to anything is up to you. The life will keep on reducing and diminishing.

Instead of allowing the time to just diminish into vanity, you can actually take that time and convert it through solitude. When you can go somewhere to go and think or use that time to study or read in the library, when you can take your time to go work in the laboratory, you are actually converting that time. You are taking advantage of every minute and you are converting it to a product. You are producing something every minute. So, that time that is pouring out, in minutes and seconds, that time that is diminishing, you are taking advantage of it. You are converting it into a product, into an invention, into a discovery, you are producing a product from it when you practice solitude.

So because you are converting it, you are actually conserving it. You are reproducing your life that way. You are not only reproducing it, you are winning back your time. You are grabbing back your life. So, instead of allowing your time to fly away, you can use it productively. For example, the person that was reading the book on the bus took advantage of his time and grabbed it back from vanity. He took it and turned it to added value into himself thereby making himself a better person. The person that is writing a book on the bus when going to work is also taking advantage of his time, not allowing his life just to be poured out or diminished. He is taking advantage of that life and converting it into another product.

To be able to convert time you must be conscious of time. Time consciousness is the key to time conversion. That is how life must be lived. You must always live in the here and now. You must live in active consciousness and what active consciousness means is that you are always asking yourself these questions" what am I doing with my life right now?" Am I using this time the best way? Am I converting it? What am I converting this time into right now? Am I converting this time into added value to myself? Am I converting it into added value to others? Am I converting the time into a product?

It is, however, alarming to find that a greater percentage of people on earth are not conscious of time hence they do not convert their time into products. No wonder our world is filled with people living in mediocrity. The very few who understand that time must be converted into products rule over the majority who are ignorant of this fact.

If you want to be among the few who rule the world you therefore must learn to convert every time of your life, every second and minute that passes by. The target of life and the idea of life is that every time must be converted into something. So begin to convert your time wisely.

SOLITUDE HELPS YOU BLOCK
TIME FROM FLYING AWAY

Solitude is what makes time conversion almost automatic. If you have an idea of what you want to do in your solitude, then solitude is actually taking the bull by the horn. Solitude is an opportunity to arrest time and convert it into products. So through solitude, you are actually blocking the way of that time that is flying away. In solitude, you are standing in the way and you are taking the bull by the horn. What you are saying is NO! I am not going to allow my life and my time just to while away like that. I am going to be battling with this time and I am going to be converting it into added value.

Whatever your decision is and whatever you decide to do in that solitude, is what you are converting that time into. You could convert the time to reading a book and acquiring knowledge. You could also convert the time into writing a book. Again you can use that time of solitude to perfect your keyboard skills or do a voice training exercise.

You could perfect your drawing skills in solitude. Whatever it is you decide to convert the time of solitude into is up to you but make sure you stand in the way of time and don't allow it fly away into vanity.

Don't join the queue of ignorant people who do not know that their time flies away into vanity daily. Don't be a part of the lazy lot who cannot discipline themselves in solitude to convert their time into products or added value. Ask yourself "What am I going to do with my life? Will I allow it keep flying away like that? If you realize that your life is diminishing per time, then you will answer those questions as soon as possible. You will hasten up to start investing your life instead of wasting it. I encourage you to start practicing solitude because the best way to convert your time into products is through solitude.

WILL YOU STILL SELL OUT YOUR LIFE?

What if I told you you've been selling out your life, would you believe me? You may want to ask" how am I selling out my life?" Well, I will be glad to tell you. Can you remember that I said earlier that time is life and life is time? Therefore when you go to work for eight hours every day, what you do is that you are pouring out eight hours of your life to that work. That is what gives you a salary. What then is salary? Salary is the compensation you get for giving out or for selling out an amount of your life. If you live in a country where you get salary daily per hour's work, then you get eight-hour compensation for your life that is being poured out for that day. I wish you knew that your life is disappearing. If you work for one month, you have given away one month of your life for a little compensation called salary. So you are selling out your life. You are selling out your life through time. You are exchanging your time for money. That is what salary is, Salary is what you get when you give out your life.

To use your life to work means giving out your time to work to get compensated for it. Why do they pay you per time, hourly or weekly, monthly or yearly? It is because your life is in time. When you dedicate one month of your life, one month of your time into a job, you get a salary for one month. When you dedicate one week of your life to a job, you get one week's salary. When you dedicate one day of your life to a job, you get one day's salary. You see, you are not just dedicating your life, you are diminishing your life. You are pouring out your life. You are giving out one week or one month of your life. Your life is disappearing but you don't know. Of course, you get a little compensation for selling out your life. That is what I call spending your life. You mortgage your life for salary. At least you mortgage something and you get something for it. So what happens when you go to work and get salary is that you are selling your life out and you are being compensated with salary. You are converting your time into salary, which is CHEAP! Which is nothin. You are actually losing your life. You are giving it out.

It is obvious that most people that are working or schooling today do not have time for solitude. They are not in control of their life. Their time is being controlled by their office boss or school management. You see, that is why it is a blessing to be fired from work. When you are fired, you become a master of your life. You will become a master of the greatest wealth that is possible; the wealth of time. You have total control of your time and you can convert it into solitude. But when you are working and you are going to work every day, you are selling out your life. You are selling out your time and you are no more the owner of your life. You have contracted your life out. Your time now is being given out to your boss. You are sold out and you are lost. You will not be able to take a hold of that time and convert it to whatever you want. You will just be using your time and your life to do what people want, to do what your boss or your company management wants. Working for your boss doesn't make you rich, it only makes your boss richer from your sweat. In the same vein, working for your government makes your government richer while you sweat out your life for a peanut salary.

But if you invest your life into yourself, you are not pouring your life out somewhere, to some job or for some salary, you are re-investing it into yourself. You are multiplying the quality of your life. When you add value to yourself, or when you convert that time into writing a book, you are multiplying your content. Your life is being multiplied. So I urge you to reconsider your life. Do you still want to sell it out or you want to invest it and reproduce it? I wish you could stop wasting your life to fulfill other people's dreams. I wish you could stop living your life for a job description. Your life was meant to be used to fulfill your purpose and destiny. Start reproducing your life. Start multiplying your life. Begin to use your life to bring out fruits and results that you desire to have. It is my desire that you consider the advice I am rendering here; that you should no longer sell your life but invest it into fulfilling the purpose for which you were born. Only then can you become great in your generation.

DON'T LIVE FOR COMPENSATION

The quality of time you dedicate to work is what determines your greatness. I do not mean working for a salary. As I have said earlier, you cannot become great by working for a salary. To work for salary is to mortgage your life. It is to give out your life for a little compensation. You were not created to live your life for compensation. You were created to invest your life into your promise land, your area of calling. You, therefore, should be working only for your purpose and area of calling. The difference between working for a salary and working for your promise land is that when you work for a salary, you are exchanging your life just for some porridge, some little compensation in the form of salary. You are giving out your life but you are getting back only compensation that is called salary. Should I remind you what salary is? Salary is the compensation you get for giving out your life. But when you choose your own land of promise, when you choose your own area of greatness, nobody determines what you earn per month or per year. When you choose your own area of calling and purpose, and you are working and converting your life into that your area of calling, you are not being compensated with salary. You become the boss over your own life. You are planting yourself and cultivating your own ground. You are investing your life into that your own land of promise.

YOUR PROMISE LAND SHOULD
BE YOUR PRIORITY

The best way to convert time is to find out your calling, find out your divine gifting and convert your time into developing your gift and your calling. What I am saying is, be intentional! Be purposeful! Bring out products in your area of calling. Maybe God wants you to bring out products in resolving medical issues or in discovery or in the computer industry or in the area of the economy, in the area of science or in politics. Just make sure you know your own calling and produce fruits in that direction.

Michelangelo, the great artistic painter we discussed earlier in this book when he goes into his studio and starts to work on his project, he remains in solitude in that studio for two months, for three months, for six months. Just painting. What was he doing? He didn't want to lose any time. He didn't want to give room for any distractions. He was taking advantage of time. He was taking the bull of time by the horns and he converted that time into the products that he wanted to see. That is why he is one of the greatest artists in history. He however produced products only in his area of calling. He was investing his own life back into his own destiny. You must understand that your calling is your destiny

He was not giving out his life to somebody to be compensated for. He was giving back his life into himself, into his own destiny and purpose. Therefore the quality of time he was able to invest into his life determined his greatness.

Michelangelo became great because of how much time he was able to invest into his promise land. For example, he will go into his land of promise and lock up himself in his studio for as much as six months. Why did he lock up himself there for such a long time? Because he didn't want time to pass by. He was converting every minute of his time into building his destiny. He didn't just want to work for eight hours per day like everyone else. He wasn't playing or joking with his destiny but was making sure none of his time was wasted and that every minute of his time was converted into greatness. If you really want to buy greatness with time, you must invest the quality amount of time into your purpose and land of calling. The more time you invest into your land of promise, the more productive the land becomes for you. So your greatness is directly proportional to how much time you are ready to invest into fulfilling your purpose. Invest maximum amount of time into refining your gift and become best at what you were called to do and you will be surprised how easily and quickly you will rise to the top. If you will invest the maximum amount of time in hard work, polishing and building your own land of promise, you will become great in life. You will become exceptional. You will become a specialist and the world would want to reckon with you.

Having read this chapter, I believe you will be more purposeful with your time. I do hope you will no longer live for compensation but begin to cultivate your own ground. Do not forget what you've just learned from this chapter. Time is the greatest wealth you have and you can turn it into a treasure called solitude. Life is about the conversion of time and the instrument to converting time is through solitude. Find out your purpose and invest your time into fulfilling it.

In the next chapter, I am going to be giving you the advantages of solitude and you will be amazed how that could change your life. Read on friends!

TIME PRINCIPLES
FROM CHAPTER SIX

1. The greatest wealth in the world is the wealth of time. There is nothing more precious than the wealth of time. If you could realize that everything is made out of time, then you can convert your free time into anything you want.

2. Solitude is the measure through which you could concentrate on using your time. It is through solitude that you can convert your time into something of value. Solitude is a way of overcoming distraction so that you can convert your time into something of worth.

3. You can really never give birth to anything in this world without solitude. Everything precious comes out of solitude.

4. Just the way a man and a woman comes together in solitude to produces a fruit, so also conception takes place when a man gets together with his creator in solitude.

5. Solitude with God is a place for pregnancy. Solitude is also a place to receive great ideas and creative ideas from God. The power of imagination is strongest in the place of solitude.

6. You must remember that whether you like it or not, every day your life is diminishing, your life is reducing and your life is pouring out. Whether you

convert that diminishing life into something or you don't convert it to anything, it's your problem. The life will keep on reducing and diminishing.

7. To be able to convert time you must be conscious of time. Time consciousness is the key to time conversion.

8. The very few who understand that time must be converted into products rule over the majority who are ignorant of this fact.

9. Whatever it is you decide to convert the time of solitude into is up to you but make sure you stand in the way of time and don't allow it fly away into vanity.

10. Don't join the queue of ignorant people who do not know that their time flies away into vanity daily. Don't be a part of the lazy lot who cannot discipline themselves in solitude to convert their time into products or added value.

HOW TO BECOME GREAT
THROUGH TIME CONVERSION

1. When you are able to overcome distractions, then you will be able to do something more specific, something more precise and definite with the time that you have.

2. If you want to give birth to any discoveries or inventions, you must start practicing solitude. If you want to give birth to your own books you must practice solitude. If you want to give birth to your own songs or musical albums, you must practice solitude. If you ever desire to give birth to anything at all, then you cannot do without solitude.

3. If you want to be among the few who rule the world you therefore must learn to convert every time of your life, every second and minute that passes by. The target of life and the idea of life is that every time must be converted into something.

4. Working for your boss doesn't make you rich, it only makes your boss richer from your sweat. In the same vein, working for your government makes your government richer while you sweat out your life for a peanut salary.

5. If you invest your life into yourself, you are not pouring your life out somewhere, to some job or for some salary, you are re-investing it into yourself. You are multiplying the quality of your life.

6. When you choose your own area of calling and purpose, and you are working and converting your life into that your area of calling, you are not being compensated with salary. You become the boss over your own life.

7. If you really want to buy greatness with time, you must invest the quality amount of time into your purpose and land of calling. The more time you invest into your land of promise, the more productive the land becomes for you.

8. So your greatness is directly proportional to how much time you are ready to invest into fulfilling your purpose.

9. It is my desire that you consider the advice I am rendering here; that you should no longer sell your life but invest it into fulfilling the purpose for which you were born. Only then can you become great in your generation.

10. If you will invest the maximum amount of time in hard work, polishing and building your own land of promise, you will become great in life. You will become exceptional. You will become a specialist and the world would want to reckon with you.

CHAPTER 7

THE ADVANTAGES
OF SOLITUDE

Dear friends, I am glad that you have followed through till this point, the truth I have been revealing to you in this book. I, however, want to state that the information you about to receive in this chapter may be the best you will ever hear on the subject of time and solitude. The ideas here can change your entire view on time and how you live your life. It is my utmost desire that you read till the end as I unveil the advantages of solitude.

REORDERING YOUR LIFE

The number one benefit of solitude is that solitude helps you to see life the way it is. Without solitude, do you know what the picture of our lives looks like? Our lives are a picture of being overwhelmed by all kind of things going on in our lives and around us. So our lives are a picture of what we ought to do, what we know we need to do, what we are planning to do and what we want to do. Without solitude, we are overwhelmed by all of the things we hope to do and all of the things we are planning and praying to do but we never really have the time to actually get down and get these things done. Life is just full of disordered pieces of unachieved plans without solitude. Without solitude, we can't fix the scattered pieces of our plans, hopes, and wishes together. No one has truly become successful without having to organize his life. With a well-organised life, you have a higher chance of success and excellence in your area of calling and in whatever you find yourself doing. Without order in your life, you will realize that you will only be busy but without commensurate results.

However, when you have solitude, you have time to just be alone with yourself and God and plan your life. Ok! What is it that I want to do? What is it that God wants me to do? How I ought to do it? When do I need to do it? Do I need to do it at all? What should I avoid doing? What is it that I must do? You see, in solitude, you are converting your time into a product of self-analysis. You get a clearer picture of what your life should be like in the place of solitude. Solitude helps you to convert your time into the clarity of purpose. Solitude gives you the opportunity to bring your life into order and helps to bring clarity into your life.

Another thing solitude does for you is that solitude allows you to just clear your mind. Because sometimes we are all mentally overwhelmed. We are overwhelmed emotionally, we are overwhelmed by what is happening around us. We are overwhelmed with all kind of information coming from left right and center. We are overwhelmed with just gathering too much information and not knowing what to do with them. We are overwhelmed by too many things we want to do that we never really get time to do. We have so much going on in our lives that we don't even have time to organize our lives. Our mind is just in a messed up state and becomes a messed up system. But our mind is supposed to be a well-planned system. Our goals and objectives are supposed to be well planned out in our minds. So solitude affords you the time to build an organized system for yourself. Solitude allows you to sit down and work out a system that works best for you.

So with solitude, you slow down and remove yourself from all the vanities of life. You remove yourself from all the distractions and all the things going on around you and just sit down and build a system for your life. If you need to invent something, for example, solitude affords you that time to go and sit down and build that system and to come out with that formula needed for your invention. Solitude allows you time to come up with an algorithm to bring forth your inventions.

> *"Order and simplification are the first steps towards mastery of a subject."*
> THOMAS MANN

Therefore with solitude, you can build a system that works for you and once you put yourself in that system, the system works for itself. The system just functions automatically and your life is reordered by it.

PRIORITIZE YOUR VALUES

The next thing that solitude will do for you is that solitude helps you put your values in place. Because you know, everything is pushing you left and right. Everything is just overwhelming you. But a time of solitude will make you come to touch with your value system. It will help you to come to touch with the things that really matter in life. It will help you come to touch with your priorities and you will be able to say "No! No! I am being distracted now. I don't want this. This is not in line with my value system. This is not valuable to me. I want to see life in the right perspective" You are able to line up your life with God's purpose for you, with God's plan for your life. You will be able to find out where you are missing it, where you are going astray from your purpose. With solitude, you will be able to find out what you are doing that is not in line with the original thought and the original mandate that you had upon your life. Solitude helps you to find out your mission, your calling, and your destiny. Solitude helps you to be able to arrange your life only around your destiny. It helps you organize the events in your life only around your calling and purpose.

SOLVING LIFE'S PROBLEMS

Whatever problem you have can be solved through solitude. I know you may not believe this. What if you are having financial problems or relationship problems? What if you are having family problems? Will solitude be of help? Yes! If you are having financial problems, for example, look for books or messages on financial freedom and wealth creation. Then lock yourself up in solitude and study and absorb all the teachings on how to create wealth. Exhaust all the materials and messages on becoming a financial giant. Write down the practical steps that you will apply once you come out of solitude and be sure to apply them so you can get the needed results. By so doing you would solve all your financial problems but thanks to the power of solitude.

Is it relationship problems? The same principles apply. Lock yourself up in solitude and absorb all the literature on relationship and marriage. Listen to all the sermons on how to enjoy a good home and a successful relation-ship with others. Then come out and apply the principles you've learned and that problem is solved. What you have done is that you have converted your time into producing a product, which is having a successful relationship with your spouse or with other people. Therefore with solitude, all problems can be solved.

Whatever topic of life that you are challenged with or that is bothering you, just take all the materials that are re-lated to that topic and go and be alone with yourself and the materials. Study them, convert them and use them to pro-duce an improved and better life in that particular area you wanted to improve. Sometimes we all need that time to just stop and take one topic, study it exhaustively and convert the topic into a product in ourselves.

> *"We cannot solve our problems with the same level of thinking that created them."*
> Albert Einstein

Doing that will help you have a new understanding of that topic and help you become an expert on that topic. You become so good in that topic and become a master in that topic. You will so know that topic that the whole world will be looking for you to solve any need they have concerning that topic.

THOMAS EDISON: CONSUMED BY HIS INVENTION

With solitude, you are able to focus and concentrate on one thing and become the best in it. It is the same thing if you want to invent something or research anything. That is exactly what Thomas Edison would do.

Thomas Alva Edison was born on February 11, 1847, in Milan, Ohio. He was the last of the seven children of Samuel and Nancy Edison. Thomas's father was a political activist while his mother was an accomplished school teacher. He suffered an early bout of scarlet fever and ear infections which resulted in hearing difficulties in both ears, and eventually left him nearly deaf as an adult.

In 1854, the family moved to Michigan, where Edison spent the rest of his childhood. He went to school only a short time. He did so poorly and was regarded as a difficult child by his teacher. He couldn't cope with school and he was withdrawn to be taught at home by his mother, a former teacher. He learned to love reading, a habit he kept for the rest of his life. He also liked to make experiments in the basement. All through his life, he was a hard worker who devoted most of his time into experimenting and giving birth to inventions. He invested his time working all night most times such that he was able to invent and develop products like the telegraph, phonograph, the electric light bulb, alkaline storage batteries and Kinetograph (a camera for motion pictures). All through his life he built several laboratories and workshops and employed several workers. But the question is "How was he able to invent and develop all these products?" The answer was simply his understanding of time conversion. He knew that time was the greatest wealth and could be converted into products. Can you imagine! Thomas Edison will go into the office {workshop} on Monday and they will come and break the door on Friday. They will come and remind him that he has not eaten and he will not even remember that it's Friday already. He thinks it's just the next day. He didn't want to waste any of his time and was converting every passing moment in that workshop experimenting and producing products. He lost touch with the environment outside his laboratory and they would break the door to get him out. That was because he was so concentrated and so focused on getting results. He would stay in solitude, doing research and converting his time into the product that he wants to create.

> *"Personally, I enjoy working about 18 hours a day. Besides the short catnaps I take each day, I average about four to five hours of sleep per night."*
> THOMAS EDISON

Did you see that! 18 hours of work per day! You cannot desire to be great when you can't even focus on 8 hours of work a day. If you want to be as great as Thomas Edison you should also be ready to invest as much time into working as he did. One of the secrets that made Thomas Edison successful was that he knew how to concentrate his time on doing just one thing. His secret to time management was *"Just focus on ONE activity"* Because he was focused on his invention alone, he got so consumed with it that he lost count of time. He didn't need to check time because he had no other job in his schedule. In fact, he had no other schedule other than his invention. For him, there was nothing to schedule because he knew always what he should be doing. You can't do everything. So choose what's important and focus on that relentlessly.

For Edison, that "one important activity" was his invention. He was legendary for working almost round the clock, sometimes working over 16hours every day just to give birth to his inventions.

Until his death on October 18, 1931{at age 84}, he was known as one who worked so hard and made sure that his time was never wasted but invested into his inventions. Before his death, everyone had heard of the "Wizard" and looked up to him. The whole world called him a genius.

By the time he died he was one of the most well-known and respected Americans in the world. He had been at the forefront of America's first technological revolution and set the stage for the modern electric world.

So my question to you is; do you want to be great? If your answer is yes, then you cannot but learn from Thomas Edison. You must learn to practice solitude like he did. You must learn to convert all your time into products via hard work. The secret of all greatness is in knowing what to do with time. You will have to stop trivializing time and learn to start investing time. Get your raw materials. Get into your laboratory. Get into your library. Get into your office or workshop and convert every passing time into tangible products and the world will soon hear your name as one of the leading specialists in your field of endeavor.

REBUILDING YOUR LIFE THROUGH SOLITUDE

Another thing you could do in your time of solitude is to rebuild your life. To rebuild your ideal life. When you are in solitude, you can do an inventory of your life. You can do a study of the most successful people in life, people that have succeeded in your area of calling. You could see what made them who they are and why they were successful. You can begin to ask yourself "what qualities do they have that I don't have?" Write down a list of the qualities they have that you have and those that they have that you don't have. Then do a study of how to get those qualities that you don't have now. Put them down and study them and meditate on them. By so doing, you will be able to bring those values and qualities that you don't have into your life. You can use that time of solitude to work on your life and rebuild yourself into the person you want to be. You can bring all those qualities and virtues to become your own through solitude, through meditation, through study, through thinking and make those qualities become flesh in you. And when they become flesh in you, you become a new man. You come out of that place a new individual, a new person altogether. You will now begin to command a new authority. You will be commanding a new power.

You can also use that time of solitude to get rid of all the bad qualities that are limiting you from fulfilling your purpose. You can get rid of all the things that are holding you back. All the weaknesses that you have. All the qualities that are not advancing you could be gotten rid of in the place of solitude. The qualities that are not propelling you forward and are not allowing you to be the best of yourself can all be uprooted from your life in the place of solitude. Then you can put in the new qualities that will make you the best anywhere in the world.

When you have the power of time and you can take possession of your time, there is nothing you cannot become. You can become anything that you want to be. But the goal is for you to become your best self. The truth is that most of us are not our best selves. Is your life now the best you can be? Is this the best your life can become? Don't you think you were created for more than this?

You see, people always get surprised when they find out where I am coming from. They say "you are coming from that village and you never had a good school. How did you become who you have become?" I made myself. I made myself who I wanted to be. I sat down and did an analysis of myself. I did an inventory of myself and I saw the things that I didn't have. I looked at other great people and saw the qualities that made them great that I was lacking. I studied more about their lives and I looked for a way to bring all those great qualities into my life. I build myself into the kind of person that I wanted to be. I created a new personality out of myself. I used to be quiet and shy. But I created a new personality that is not shy, that is not limited and that is not intimidated. I discovered that I was not bold and I built boldness in my character through solitude. I was always holding back but I built myself to become an upstart and a proactive person. I created that value in myself. I used to be afraid of smiling in public and I created a lively person out of myself because I know that lively people are more interesting and they always get things done easily. So I created myself.

I didn't like being alone. I was always afraid of being alone and so after I discovered the importance of solitude, I forced myself, to create the habit of being alone and being in solitude. Because I knew that I needed it. So I rebuilt myself. Listen to me! You can actually remold yourself. You can remodel yourself to anything you want to become.

One of the most important things you could actually do in life is to create the best of yourself, to create your ideal self. What you are seeing now, you are assuming that that is you. I know you are thinking "But this is just who I am" No! That is not who you are. You can be better than that. Just imagine this: If you had been born from the same parent and you were given birth to in another country; let's say you are living right now in England but you were given birth to in America. You will be speaking another language, I mean you will be speaking with another accent. Because of the environment, because of the school and because of the people you met, your character will be different, your attitude will be different and your reactions will be different. Even though your name is still the same, even though you are coming from the same parent. Or let's say you were born in South Africa but you have European parents. But because you were born there, the people you were exposed to, the lifestyle you were exposed to, the language they speak, the values you were thought, all made you who you are. So you see, we are all products of accidents. We are all products of the failures of the people who raised us up. We are products of the lack of understanding of the people who raised us up. We are products of their wisdom or lack of wisdom, their understanding or lack of understanding. We are products of their weaknesses or their strengths. We are all a whole bunch of accidental products. We are all products of incidence. But instead of you to just be at the mercy of whatever they have made you into; what your school has made you into, what your country has made you into, and what your parents have made you into, rebuild your life into what it should be. Don't just remain that accidental product. Don't just remain an accidental being. Take that your accidental self and build it into your ideal self. Create the best out of yourself. Become your best self. But remember, this can only be possible through the power of solitude.

From the foregoing, you can see that it is not just products that you can produce through solitude. You can also produce your best self. Once you have produced your best self, then you will be able to produce new seeds and fruits after your kind.

ELIMINATE THE FEARS AND WORRIES

Another thing that solitude will do for you is that you can use the time of solitude to get rid of worries. You can get rid of anxieties through the power of solitude. Even fear can be eliminated through solitude. You can come into the peace of God through solitude. You can come into the rest of God through solitude because Christ Jesus is our rest. So you can use the time of solitude to get rid of all the junks in your life. You can get rid of all the worries and fears in your life. You can actually be in a solitude with an assignment to get rid of all fears, never to fear again in your life. So you get hold of all the materials and books that talk about how to overcome fear. You go and get all the messages that talk about faith and belief in yourself and listen to them. You exhaust the materials and work out how to get rid of your fears before you come out of that solitude. So that by the time you come out of that solitude nobody can recognize you again. You would have turned your timid and fearful self into somebody that is violently bold. Sometimes when people listen to me, they say "we cannot understand where your boldness is coming from" They say that my boldness is intimidating and that my boldness is almost becoming violent. Well, it is because I created this in myself. I created this by converting the time of solitude into the character and quality that I needed. Characters that I didn't have before became mine thanks to solitude.

The time of solitude should, therefore, be used to convert time into products. The shirt you are wearing is a product of time. If nobody spent the time to produce it, then it wouldn't exist and you wouldn't have it. This book you are reading now is a product of time because somebody took the time to write it. The iPad you are using is a product of time. People took the time to produce it. Everything is a product of time. You too can use your time to produce anything you want. Either you produce in yourself by adding value to yourself or produce in others by teaching them or writing books for them to read. And you could actually produce tangible products through the conversion of time. You can convert time into any product that you wish to have.

DEPENDING ON YOUR SOURCE

Another thing that solitude will do for you is that it will help you to be dependent on God. When you are always surrounded by people, you begin to think that you need people to survive. You think that without your parents or without your husband or your wife and children you cannot survive. But in the place of solitude, you are alone with yourself and with God. When you are alone with your vision, your projects and your plans, you discover all of a sudden that you are alone there and you are surviving and you just want to depend on God while you are there. Solitude helps you discover that you can walk through life all by yourself and that you don't need to be dependent on anything. You begin to realize that you don't need to be addicted to anything. You come to understand that you don't need to be dependent on people to become who God has made you be. You can become everything you need all by yourself. In solitude, you just begin discovering the one who created you, the one from whom you came. If you can just discover him, he will become your sole source.

> *"Bread is a second cause; the LORD Himself is the first source of our sustenance. He can work without the second cause as well as with it, and we must not tie Him down to one mode of operation. Let us not be too eager after the visible, but let us look to the invisible God."*
> CHARLES HADDON SPURGEON

It is a great thing to be able to make God your source and the time of solitude presents you with that opportunity. This means that the time of solitude sets you free and makes you less dependent on people, less dependent on job and less dependent on things. You can just use solitude time to set yourself free from dependency. Because dependency on stuff, on people and on things is one of the greatest things that could kill. It could enslave you and put you in bondage. But with solitude, you change yourself into someone who is only dependent on God.

BECOME FREE FROM THE RAT RACE

Another thing solitude will give you is that it will set you free from the rat race of life. The rat race of life is just crazy. You want to be like everybody else, you want to copy everybody else. You want to get that car because everybody else is having the car. You want to build that house because everybody else is building a house. You want to work more, you want to get salary and you want to get a promotion. All kind of rat race, deceptions of life and vanity of life. You can set yourself free from the vanity of life and just concentrate on one or two things or maybe three things that matter in life. Just focus on the things that you are called to do in life. Focus on your purpose and your destiny and just be a free person. Like I said before you can't do everything. So pick what's important and focus on that relentlessly.

Finally, solitude helps you to be more efficient and proficient. Because in the time of solitude you are not being distracted with telephone calls, with friends or with social media. You are focusing and concentrating and that makes you more efficient than when you are just living your regular haphazard life. So solitude time is a time of concentrated actions and concentrated results. If there is anything you need more than anything else to succeed in life, it is solitude. Make solitude your way of life and greatness will naturally become yours.

Dear friends, I told you from the beginning of this chapter that the information you will get here may be the best you would ever get on the subject matter. I believe now it is clear to you that you can recreate or rebuild your life to become your best self through the power of time conversion in solitude. I believe you can apply solitude now to solve any problem that you are faced with. I am hoping that you will learn to become focus like Thomas Edison by investing your time into one or two things that pattern to your purpose and calling in life. It is my utmost desire that you don't just read this book but apply the principles that are therein.

In the next chapter, I am about to reveal a secret that most great men have used to buy their greatness. It is called The Rule of Ten Thousand Hours. Proceed with me dear friends as the next chapter could turn your whole life around for good.

TIME PRINCIPLES
FROM CHAPTER SEVEN

1. The number one benefit of solitude is that solitude helps you to see life the way it is.

2. Life is just full of disordered pieces of unachieved plans without solitude. Without solitude, we can't fix the scattered pieces of our plans, hopes, and wishes together.

3. No one has truly become successful without having to organize his life.

4. Without order in your life, you will realize that you will only be busy but without commensurate results.

5. You get a clearer picture of what your life should be like in the place of solitude. Solitude helps you to convert your time into the clarity of purpose.

6. Solitude allows you to sit down and work out a system that works best for you.

7. Solitude allows you time to come up with an algorithm to bring forth your inventions.

8. With solitude, you will be able to find out what you are doing that is not in line with the original thought and the original mandate that you had upon your life.

9. Solitude helps you to find out your mission, your calling, and your destiny.

10. Solitude helps you to be able to arrange your life only around your destiny. It helps you organise the events in your life only around your calling and purpose.

HOW TO BECOME GREAT
THROUGH TIME CONVERSION

1. If you are having financial problems, for example, look for books or message on financial freedom and wealth creation. Then lock yourself up in solitude and study and absorb all the teachings on how to create wealth.

2. Exhaust all the materials and messages on becoming a financial giant. Write down the practical steps that you will apply once you come out of solitude and be sure to apply them so you can get the needed results.

3. Lock yourself up in solitude and absorb all the literature on relationship and marriage. Listen to all the sermons on how to enjoy a good home and a successful relationship with others. Then come out and apply the principles you've learnt and that problem is solved.

4. Whatever topic of life that you are challenged with or that is bothering you, just take all the materials that are related to that topic and go and be alone with yourself and the materials. Study them, convert them and use them to produce an improved and better life in that particular area you wanted to improve.

5. With solitude, you are able to focus and concentrate on one thing and become the best in it.

6. Get your raw materials. Get into your laboratory. Get into your library. Get into your office or workshop and convert every passing time into tangible products and the world will soon hear your name as one of the leading specialists in your field of endeavour.

7. Another thing you could do in your time of solitude is to rebuild your life. To rebuild your ideal life.

8. You can also use that solitude to get rid of all the bad qualities that are limiting you from fulfilling your purpose.

9. When you have the power of time and you can take possession of your time, there is nothing you cannot become. You can become anything that you want to be. But the goal is for you to become your best self.

10. Don't just remain an accidental being. Take that your accidental self and build it into your ideal self. Create the best out of yourself. Become your best self. But remember, this can only be possible through the power of solitude.

CHAPTER 8

THE RULE OF TEN THOUSAND HOURS

People have often wondered how some great men in the past have gained mastery over their skills and talents and became great through that. Most times we even think that those who have become exceptionally good at what they do are geniuses and are almost tempted to worship them. In this chapter, I am going to prove to you that you too can become the great genius that will astound everyone else. I want to show you that geniuses are not born, they are made and the rule through which they gain mastery is what I am about to reveal to you.

GIVE ME THREE YEARS

With the power of solitude, you can actually take up a decision to invent anything. With the power of solitude, you can decide to become the best in the world in any area of life you choose and it will happen. If you could invest ten thousand hours into discovering anything, if you could invest ten thousand hours into studying and adding value to yourself, if you invest ten thousand hours into anything through solitude, if you could convert that amount of time into practising and working on something, whatsoever it is, you will become one of the best in the world in that field.

Ten thousand hours converted into researching and rehearsing anything will turn you into a world best achiever in that field of endeavour. This theory was proposed by **Malcolm Gladwell** and has been proven in history. Anybody that dedicates ten thousand hours doing anything repeatedly becomes one of the best in that thing. For example, the Singapore swimmer, **Joseph schooling** in the 2016 Olympic Games, who overcame and beat his idol **Michael Phelps,** only spent eight years rehearsing and practising swimming three hours every day and that made him better than his idol; Michael Phelps whom he used to admire.

They have known each other for a long time. They first met in 2008, when the US team stopped off in Singapore for a training camp before the Beijing Games. Schooling who was then 13years old was so excited to have met one on one with his hero. Narrating the remarkable incidence, Schooling said "They came to the country club that I trained at. It was early in the morning, and he was working on an essay. Everyone just rushed up and was like "it's Michael Phelps! It's Michael Phelps!' and I really wanted a picture. Phelps obliged. And I was so shell shocked, I couldn't really open my mouth".

Joseph schooling did not just stop at admiring and wishing to become like his hero Michael Phelps. He didn't just live in the world of wishes. He converted his time into becoming what he wished for. He invested his time into becoming great. Joseph understood that through the power of time conversion anyone could become great. He knew that just by applying the principle of time conversion you can become better and greater than your idols and heroes. With this understanding, Joseph disciplined himself to practise swimming three hours every day for eight years. Can you imagine that! Such a discipline; converting three hours every day for eight years into perfecting his swimming skills. Eight years later Joseph schooling met his idol again but this time it is not to ask him for a picture nor an autograph. The 13year old Joseph has become 21year old now. The past eight years did not just vanish into vanity. No! Joseph arrested the time and reproduced it into added value to himself. He converted that passing time into perfecting his swimming skills.

> *"The only competition that matters the most, is competing to become better than your best old self."*
> EDMOND MBIAKA

So now he is meeting his idol not as a fan but as a rival. This time Joseph Schooling was meeting his idol {Michael Phelps} on the world stage to compete with him at the 2016 Olympics.

I guess you know how the story ended. This was how the news captured it " Eight years later, Schooling's winning time of 50.39 sec broke the Olympic record Phelps set at those same Beijing Games" They say you shouldn't meet your heroes. Schooling beat his. How did it happen? The answer is **TIME CONVERSION.** If you devote three to six hours of your time every day to practising anything repeatedly, in the next five years, you will become one of the best in the world. Why? Because the world doesn't know how to concentrate. The world doesn't know how to concentrate on working.

"In the future, the great division will be between those who have trained themselves to handle these complexities and those who are overwhelmed by them — those who can acquire skills and discipline their minds and those who are irrevocably distracted by all the media around them and can never focus enough to learn."

Robert Greene, Mastery

Most of the people in the world are just distracted and work only on the surface. But if you will be deep enough to concentrate and study or rehearse anything, the world will bow in honour to you. The whole world will stand still to give you a way to the top if you practise the rule of ten thousand hours. The world gives way to the man who knows where he is going. If you can take ten thousand hours and divide it by the number of hours you can concentrate and devote to repeatedly doing one single thing in a day, you will be amazed how good you will become in that thing after a given number of years.

It is from your time that wealth is produced. It is the conversion of time that produces results and products. So if you could dedicate six hours, for example, every day or eight hours every day just practising one thing repeatedly, or developing one thing or researching and perfecting your act in one thing, I bet you, in the next four to five years you will become the world best in that thing. It doesn't matter what that thing is; it could be in music, in dancing, in medicine, in engineering, in soccer or in swimming, whatever it is; the rule of ten thousand hours will make you the world best in three years, in four years or in five years depending on how many hours you spend practising that thing a day.

How can you do that? You can only do that through the power of solitude. You can only become great through the power of time conversion.

If you decide to practise something repeatedly 8 hours every day, it will take you only about three years to become a genius in that thing. Do I have people in Nigeria who will say, GIVE ME THREE YEARS, and I will become the world best in singing, give me three years, and I will become the world best in soccer or in swimming? Are there people in Africa who will challenge the world and say give me just three years and I will become the world best Olympic athlete or the best footballer in the world? The church can raise champions from Nigeria who will become the best in medical research and discoveries in a matter of three years if this rule is practised. The world best guitarist can arise from Nigeria if he engages this rule. We can raise the best software designers from Nigeria. If there is anyone who truly desires to be great in Africa, this is the fastest route to achieving greatness. If there are people in Nigeria who desire to climb the world stage and be reckoned among the world best in any field of endeavour, then they cannot but engage the rule of ten thousand hours. Do you really want to become great? Then you have to practise the rule of ten thousand hours. You have to learn to convert your time daily in solitude. You have to get rid of every form of distraction and begin to invest your life. If you can practise the rule of ten thousand hours, you will be amazed to find out how easy it is to become the best in that your area of calling.

THE CHILDREN OF SOLITUDE

The best way to practise the rule of ten thousand hours is through solitude. Remember what I said before, that everything precious comes out of solitude. For example, all the books I have written were born out of solitude. There are no great writers that write great books without being in solitude. There are no book authors who never invested their time into solitude. The act of writing books itself is for you to be alone with your thoughts and be able to transfer your thoughts into a substance. So the book is a result of solitude. When you go into solitude, solitude always gives birth to something. Just the way solitude gives birth to pregnancy and every child is born out of solitude, so it is with every precious thing on the earth; they all come into existence thanks to solitude. Therefore, solitude always gives birth to a seed. Solitude will always give birth to a product. The IPad you use is as a result of solitude. The phone you use is as a result of solitude. The cars you drive are born out of solitude. Nobody can come up with the idea of the IPad without being alone with his thought and putting it down. Nobody can come up with a manufactured car without first of all drawing the design in the place of solitude. So, in the place of solitude, you are able to take advantage of time and bring forth children in the form of products. You just don't allow time to while away but you take hold of time and make a demand on it to bring forth offspring. Offspring of improved knowledge, offspring of added value, offspring of books written, offspring of music albums, offspring of cars, offspring of phones and offspring of iPads. You can give birth to anything in solitude be it in technology, in medicine, in art, in economics or in the computer world. Solitude will always produce children. All the medical discoveries in the past were children of solitude. All the radiological discoveries in the past were offspring of solitude. The latest discoveries in science and technology were possible only thanks to solitude. Even you reading this book were born out of solitude. This means that whenever you make up your mind to go into solitude, you must decide first of all what you want to go and do there. You must be definite about what kind of child you want to give birth to from solitude.

A time of solitude could be used for different things. It could be used for producing something. It could be used for giving birth to ideas or giving birth to products. It could be a time of enriching yourself and adding value to yourself. Solitude could also be a time of releasing the virtues that are already in you, turning them into some products or service. It could also be a time of research.

Solitude gives birth to greatness. All the great names you know, like Michelangelo, Salvador Dali etc. all invested their time to produce products that made them great. They go into a time of solitude and they sit there in solitude for six months, sometimes one year, two years and three years in solitude. They all practised the rule of ten thousand hours. In fact, when I got to saint Basilica church in Vatican city in Rome, I heard that some of these great people were in that saint Basilica for three years, four years, or six years in solitude. They just bring them food to eat and they go to the rest room. They remained in solitude for such an amount of time, but not just in solitude meditating or just wasting away life again. They were in solitude fulfilling destiny.

They were in solitude producing and converting time into products.

Most religious people go into solitude with no specific goal of what they want to achieve through the solitude. That is a total waste of time. Do not go into solitude if you do not have an aim. Do not go into solitude because everyone else is doing that. It will be a waste of time to lock up yourself in isolation if you do not have a plan of what you want to achieve. The great artists of old went into solitude with specific intentions and hence came out with specific products. So you must be intentional and decisive about what you want to achieve during your solitude time. That is the key to productivity.

JOHANN SEBASTIAN BACH: BECOME CRAZILY PRODUCTIVE

The great music composer, **Johann Sebastian Bach** is considered today as one of the greatest Western composers of all time. Johann Sebastian, born 1685, in Eisenach in Thuringia, where his father was court organist. He grew up in an atmosphere of good music having been born into a family of musicians. Can you believe that he started having solitude from the age of 9! Sebastian was only ten years old when he lost his parents. The young orphan became dependent on his elder brother, Johann Christoph, who was an organist. Sebastian started his first lessons in singing and playing the clavichord with his elder brother.

Sebastian who loved investing his time into practising the art of playing the clavichord was however allowed to practise for just one hour a day. This was because his elder brother and the wife didn't want to be disturbed by too much practising. Also, his older brother prohibited him from using his well-furnished musical library for practises and hid the key to the book case in his own pocket. However little Sebastian was too passionate about music that he would manage to pick the lock in the night when everyone was asleep. He would tip-toe downstairs in his bare feet and get a sheet of music and copy it by moonlight sitting on the window sill. He continued this for almost six months until he was caught and punished. That, however, did not deter him but rather fuelled his love for music. So Sebastian became a voracious lover of music.

Sebastian Bach invested all of his life into the art of music. He constantly improved his skills in composing and playing music. He understood the importance of time conversion and made sure he never wasted time on things that were not connected to his musical calling. He practised the rule of ten thousand hours and gained the mastery over his musical skills and talents. He became the choirmaster and musical director of two churches St. Nicholas and St. Thomas in Leipzig.

He converted so much time perfecting his skills and talents until he became so skilful that he was considered as the founder of the *modern art of piano playing*, as he was the first to insist upon equal use of the thumb with the rest of the hand and to act upon the principle that touch proceeds from the lower joints of the fingers and not from the wrist or arms. He was said to have played with so much ease and skill that the movement of his fingers was hardly perceptible. His playing was light, smooth, swift — powerful or expressive as he chose — but always without display or the appearance of effort.

No man can be as skilful as Bach without first investing his time into relentless rehearsals. Self-improvement is possible only through time conversion in solitude. He converted his time into added value to himself and that reflected in the number of products he was able to produce.

He had so many materials produced from his converted time such that we could say he was the most productive person that ever lived. By the time he was dead, they found his works and hired a secretary to just rewrite and copy, just to copy what he has done. It took more than seventy years to be able to copy what he has been able to produce. It was almost as if he was producing products per minute of his life. He was so productive that one could assume he never had any distractions.

> *"...The good life warrants an ongoing struggle to be clear about what's important, and to seek it with lucidity and passion; not to be distracted by false ambitions, or waylaid by dissipated conscious."*
> DAMON YOUNG

He must have overcome all his distractions to the extent that solitude became his way of life. The only avenue through which a man could be as productive as Sebastian Bach would be through solitude. Solitude makes you productive like crazy. He was converting every minute of his life. He only lived for 65years but it took more than 70years to rewrite the works he produced. Can you imagine that! He didn't even live up to the amount of time needed to rewrite his works. People were working full time to rewrite his works and they took over seventy years to complete it.

Just to rewrite his works took that long, what about him that created that work? He didn't waste his time like most people do. He was using every minute, he was converting every minute of his life into products. To become as crazily productive like Sebastian Bach you must convert every minute of your time. You must overcome every distraction and isolate yourself in solitude making sure that every time that passes is converted into some products.

YOU CAN BE AS PRODUCTIVE AS SEBASTIAN BACH

If you ever desire to gain the mastery over any skill and talent then you must convert as much time as Bach converted. If you really want to live a productive life and saturate the earth with your products, then you must learn from the life of Sebastian Bach. His secret was the rule of ten thousand hours. His secret was that he converted so much time into improving himself and becoming the master of his career.

Our world is filled with people who have only a shallow knowledge of certain skills and have remained like that for so many years without self-improvement. Most people have not become better than they were five years ago. The reason is because people hardly invest time into improving their knowledge, skills, and talents. To truly be better than your past self, you must practise the rule of ten thousand hours and you must invest so much time building yourself up. You will be amazed at what capacities you have unused by the time you start practising self-improvement. You can be the most productive person in your area of your calling if you can just isolate yourself and learn to convert your time into products. You can be as productive as Bach. The secret is time conversion.

"Make use of time, let not advantage slip."
WILLIAM SHAKESPEARE

That is why when people ask me, how come I have written three hundred books? My response is this; it is about taking advantage of time. It is by being able to overcome the distractions of life and by converting time into products. It is by realizing that time is the wealth from which everything comes.

So solitude allows you without any distraction to convert your time into products. Your ability to overcome distractions will determine how long you can stay in solitude. In solitude, when you are converting time, you need a high level of concentration for you to read and not to be distracted. You need a high level of concentration for you to write and not to be distracted. Therefore you must learn focus and concentration for you to enjoy solitude.

Summarizing this chapter, I want to remind you that you can become the best in the world in any area of life you choose if only you will practise the rule of ten thousand hours. Solitude is a precious time and through it, you can invest ten thousand hours and gain the mastery over any skill or talent you have. You can become your best self and be better than your idols and heroes like Joseph schooling did if you practise the rule of ten thousand hours. With solitude, you can become as productive as Johann Sebastian Bach and convert your time into products. That is why I said solitude is a treasure. You should actually be fighting to have a time of solitude because, through it, you can make yourself great.

Dear friends, in the next chapter I am going to be showing you how to convert your time into money. I invite you to proceed with me to learn how money can be made from time conversion.

TIME PRINCIPLES
FROM CHAPTER EIGHT

1. Ten thousand hours converted into researching and rehearsing anything will turn you into a world best achiever in that field of endeavour.

2. It is from your time that wealth is produced. It is the time that produces results and products.

3. Most of the people in the world are just distracted and work only on the surface. But if you will be deep enough to concentrate and study or rehearse anything, the world will bow in honour to you.

4. If you can practise the rule of ten thousand hours, you will be amazed to find out how easy it is to become the best in that your area of calling.

5. When you go into solitude, solitude always gives birth to something. Just the way solitude gives birth to pregnancy and every child is born out of solitude, so it is with every precious thing on the earth; they all come into existence thanks to solitude.

6. In the place of solitude, you are able to take advantage of time and bring forth children in the form of products.

7. Solitude gives birth to greatness. All the great names you know, like Michelangelo, Salvador Dali etc. all invested their time to produce products that made them great.

8. Solitude allows you without any distraction
   to convert your time into products.

9. You should actually be fighting to have
   a time of solitude because through it,
   you can make yourself great.

10. You need a high level of concentration
    for you to write and not to be distracted.
    Therefore you must learn focus and
    concentration for you to enjoy solitude.

HOW TO BECOME GREAT
THROUGH TIME CONVERSION

1. The whole world will stand still to give you
    a way to the top if you practise the rule of
    ten thousand hours. The world gives way to
    the man who knows where he is going.

2. If you can take ten thousand hours and divide it
    by the number of hours you can concentrate and
    devote to repeatedly doing one single thing in a
    day, you will be amazed how best you will become
    in that thing after a given number of years.

3. Do you really want to become great? Then you have
    to practise the rule of ten thousand hours. You have
    to learn to convert your time daily in solitude.

4. Don't allow time to while away but take hold of time
    and make a demand on it to bring forth offspring.

5. If you could dedicate six hours, for example,
    every day, or eight hours every day just practising
    one thing repeatedly, or developing one thing
    or researching and perfecting your act in one
    thing, I bet you, in the next four to five years
    you will become the world best in that thing.

6. You have to get rid of every form of
    distraction and begin to invest your life.

7. You can give birth to anything in solitude be it in technology, in medicine, in art, in economics or in the computer world.

8. Whenever you make up your mind to go into solitude, you must decide first of all what you want to go and do there. You must be definite about what kind of child you want to give birth to from this solitude.

9. Your ability to overcome distractions will determine how long you can stay in solitude.

10. To become as crazily productive like Sebastian Bach you must convert every minute of your time.

CHAPTER 9

MONEY IS MADE OUT OF TIME

Dear Readers, can you imagine waking up this morning and credited to your account is $86,400 USD. However, you only have 24 hours to spend it.

Just like the biblical manna from heaven, this blessing works by the same principle. By the time you go back to bed, 12 midnight, whatever money you have not spent would be wiped out off your account. By 6 am the next morning, you will be credited with another $86,400 USD and at 12 midnight your account will again be emptied.

That is exactly the amount of wealth God gives to each and every one of us on a daily basis. God has made the provision for every man on earth to be equally endowed with this currency. So in actual fact, every human being is equally wealthy according to God's divine Providence.

The wealth I am referring to is the wealth of TIME. It is the only wealth every human being comes to the earth with. We are all endowed with the wealth of time equally. Everybody that is born on the surface of this earth, has this wealth.

> *"Time is really the only capital that any*
> *human being has, and the only thing he*
> *can't afford to lose."*
> THOMAS EDISON

When people talk about starting a business the first thing they think they require is money. Everyone thinks money is the capital needed to start up a business or any project of choice. I, however, disagree with that ideology. Money is not the capital that you need. Time is the real capital that anyone needs to start up any project. The lack of this understanding is the reason why people value money but trivialize time. Everything comes out of time like I have stated before in this book, therefore, time is the real capital. Time is, therefore, the greatest wealth in the world and only through conversion of time can money be made.

Ladies and gentlemen, this wealth of time is actually of more value than natural resources (petroleum, gold, diamond, gas etc.). It is the only wealth that is more valuable than human resources. The resource of time is the ultimate resource. Time is the ultimate wealth.

You may ask "How could time be more valuable than human resource? Oh, yea! The reason is because a human resource is limited to the duration of his/ her lifespan, while time is unlimited.

> *"Being rich is having money; being wealthy*
> *is having time."*
> MARGARET BONNANO

Now, let me unveil the riddle to you. The $86,400 USD I mentioned above is actually the number of seconds we all have in a day. That amount of seconds God credits to each and every one of us daily. But when you go to bed it is wiped out and you get another one credited to you when you wake up.

The only difference is that in the analogy I gave above, I refer to the figure 86,400 as if it were in US dollars, but in the real sense, it is much more serious than that. It is not USD that is been jeopardized on daily basis, it is actually 86,400 seconds of your life. You are given that amount of life every day in time, not in dollars. That amount of time is to be converted into some products, benefits, goods, services, welfare, ministry, but most of us actually truncate this amount of wealth on daily basis.

There is no other continent in the world where time is wasted like it is wasted in Africa. The wealth of time we waste in Africa is worth much more than all the natural resources we have on the continent. The slow rate of development in almost every sector of Nigeria, for example, could attest to the fact that Africans do not know how to invest time and convert it into products. The recession and regression of any society are always an indication of how poorly the citizens of that country understand the value of time. Why are we not having the rise of indigenous petroleum industries and Gold mining companies all over the country? Why is it that we still import plastic products and electronics from china and Japan? Why has our country become a dumping ground for any kind of products from the western world? Is it not obvious that these nations have better converted their time into products than Nigeria? It is because of how we trivialize and waste time in Nigeria that we don't have any product to show for our time. We have become an importing country simply because we do not have products to export. The reason is simple, we do not convert time into products. Nigerians will rather waste time in churches and in the pub than invest it in the laboratory doing research. Nigerians can waste two hours every other day of the week at sports cinemas watching football matches but cannot invest just two hours a day in the library studying. You will be amazed that a whole year could pass with some Africans never opening a book to read that could improve their knowledge and added value. Little wonder, the majority of people in Africa are poor and are barely struggling to survive. Why wouldn't we be a poor continent financially and developmentally when we do not convert our time into wealth!

BILL GATES BECAME RICH
THROUGH TIME CONVERSION

The continents that understand that money is made out of time have judiciously invested their time into generating wealth. The avenue through which they got their money is via time conversion. Most citizens in the western countries have learnt how to isolate themselves and think. They know how to meditate and generate ideas that could change the world for good. Can you believe this! Recently I was listening to **Bill Gates** and he said there is one thing he cannot miss. He said from the time of his youth he has been practising solitude. He said he takes two weeks every year just to be alone in solitude, with no human being around. He comes out of solitude with an innovative idea which is then converted into a tangible product. That product is then converted to money. So you see, Bill Gates practised time conversion and that is what made him the Bill Gates the whole world is celebrating. He became the renowned Bill Gates through the power of conversion in solitude. He became world's richest man thanks to his understanding of the wealth of time. He became world richest man because he understood that money could be made out of time. He converted his time into products because he knew that money is made only from a time well converted. He is not even a believer. He doesn't believe in God, yet he understands the power of time conversion. Solitude is a law that works for you no matter what. The law of conversion of time will work for you anytime. Whether you are a believer or not, solitude will give you the same result. Like I said before, the greatest wealth in the world is time. So he is converting time into a product that later gives him money. Therefore money is made out of time. Money is a by-product of time. Money is just time that is well converted. Therefore time is the raw material from which money is made. Time is the raw material from which products are made and when products are sold, money is made. Time is the raw material from which everything comes. But only when that time is converted can you produce something from it. You can only make money from a time well converted.

Time is the wealth through which money comes. It is the wealth through which everything comes into existence.

WHY NO AFRICAN IS ON THE LIST OF THE TOP TEN RICHEST MEN IN THE WORLD

I have seen the list of the top ten richest men in the world from the year 2000 until the year 2016 and I was not surprised to not find the name of an African on that list. I mean for sixteen good years, no African could inscribe his name on the list of the top ten richest men in the world. What a shame! What a disgrace! I am talking about a continent of over fifty four countries with a population of over 1.1 billion people. To not have a man from Africa who could rank among the top ten richest people in the world should be a thing of concern for our continent. The question however is; why can't an African be on that list! The answer is TIME, the understanding of how to convert time into products. Like I said before, Africa has gotten no competitive products and I have said before in this book that products are only gotten from a time well converted and that financial wealth is a product of time. Our failure to convert time into products is the reason why no African is on the list.

Permit me to highlight the names on the list for the 2016 real time rating {December 13, 2016} of the top ten richest men in the world.

1. **Bill Gates** of the United States is first on the list with a net worth of 83.8 billion USD and his source of wealth is his product Microsoft.

2. **Warren Buffet** of the United States is second on the list with a net worth of 74.4 billion USD and his source of wealth is his product, Berkshire Hathaway.

3. **Amancio Ortega** of Spain is third on the list with a net worth of 72.8 billion USD and his source of wealth is his product Zara clothing (Inditex fashion group}

4. **Jeff Bezos** of the United States occupies the fourth position on the list with a net worth of 65.7 billion USD and his source of wealth is his product Amazon.com.

5. The young American **Mark Zuckerberg** is fifth on the list with a net worth of 50 billion USD and his source of wealth is his product Facebook.

6. **Larry Ellison** of the United States is sixth on the list with a net worth of 49.9 billion USD and his source of wealth is his product Oracle.

7. **Carlos Slim Helu** of Mexico occupies the seventh position with a net worth of 49.8 billion USD and his source of wealth is his product telecom.

8. **Charles Koch** of the United States is on the eight position with a net worth of 43.8 billion USD and his source of wealth is his product diversified {Koch Industries}

9. **David Koch** of the United States is also on the eight position with his brother Charles with a net worth of 43.8 billion USD and his source of wealth is his product diversified{Koch Industries}

10. **Michael Bloomberg** of the United States in on the ninth position with a net worth of 41.9 billion USD and his source of wealth is his product Bloomberg Lp.

Looking at this list, you will realise that everyone here has a product to offer to the world. In other words, they all converted their time into some kind of products for which the world pays them money. We could say therefore that their wealth is a product of the time they converted into products. No man can come up with the idea of the products listed above without first investing time into studying, thinking and meditating. Even after the idea is birthed in the place of solitude and time conversion, time is also required to convert all ideas and added values into the tangible products that benefit the world. Therefore these people are not rich because they have money, they are rich because they converted time into products. Why is there no African on that list! Because Africans do not know what to do with time. We do not know how to invest time. We need to learn how to convert time into products.

If you desire to be financially wealthy but don't know how to invest time, then you are just dreaming. To confess greatness and financial prosperity will be a joke if you still waste time and spend time on non-productive events. If you really want to be financially wealthy you must begin to convert your time into producing something for the world. The world only gives money to those who have converted their time into products. The world doesn't give money to those who spend 24hrs in Church everyday praying for financial miracles. People do not become world richest men by praying but by time conversion into products. No man has become world richest man because he wasted his time in the pub or in the cinemas watching movies and sports. No man has been rewarded world richest man for sleeping away his time every day and night. Those who have made it to the top have only done so through hard work and time conversion. Remember, greatness is bought with time and so is financial prosperity!

CONQUERING YOUR TERRITORY THROUGH TIME CONVERSION

In life, everyone must decide in what area of life he or she wants to be great. You must choose what territory you want to conquer. After deciding the territory you want to rule over, the next thing you must do is to invest your time into developing yourself and becoming the best in that territory. This means that you must convert all of your minutes and seconds into adding value to yourself in that field. To become the king of that territory you must not allow any of your time pass without converting it into building your skills in that area of life. You must arrest every passing time and convert it into growing your knowledge and prowess in that chosen field of influence. If you allow someone else to convert more time than you in your chosen territory, you automatically become a servant or a second class citizen in that territory and whoever it is who converted more time than you in that territory becomes your king and will lord it over you in that territory.

If you don't want to just live an ordinary life, then you will have to be intentional about converting all your time into that which you have been called to do. You must, first of all, evolve the consciousness of being the best in whatever territory you choose to explore and then invest all your time into it and you will be amazed how easy it is to become great. It doesn't matter what your calling is, if you can invest all your time into it then greatness will become your reward.

> *"If a man is called to be a street sweeper,*
> *he should sweep streets even as a*
> *Michelangelo painted, or Beethoven*
> *composed music or Shakespeare wrote*
> *poetry. He should sweep streets so well that*
> *all the hosts of heaven and earth will pause*
> *to say, 'Here lived a great street sweeper*
> *who did his job well."*
> MARTIN LUTHER KING JR.

Therefore the way to becoming the best in your area of calling is to invest more time than anyone else in that area of life. So you must decide what territory you want to conquer and give it all of your time.

Bill gates decided to rule over the world of software development and the world is enjoying Microsoft today. Can you imagine what the world will be like without Microsoft! Can you imagine what our school system will be like if there were no Microsoft in our world today! What about the banking sector, the finance sector, the internet world etc. There is almost no area of life that doesn't need Microsoft word, office or PowerPoint today. But you see, the world is enjoying Microsoft because somebody invested his time into developing a software and today he rules over that territory. Bill Gates doesn't have to look for a government job or wait for a government salary to survive. He is the boss and lord over his territory and the richest man in the world. But how did he become lord over money too? He did that just by converting his time into money. So don't forget "money is made out of time"

Steve Jobs decided to rule over the world of microcomputers {phones and minicomputers} and today the world is enjoying iPhone, iPad, Apple store and all other apple products. Can you imagine how the world will look like without these products? Steve Jobs is dead but his products live on in the hands of almost everyone alive today. Why is it so? Because he produced the best phone product for the world. He didn't just produce a normal product like other producers in his field. He invested time into producing the best. The amount of time you invest into your products determines the quality of the products. The latest iPhone was just released recently and the whole world is craving to buy it. Why are people ready to buy his iPhone at a very high cost when there are other cheaper brands of phones in the market? Why are people using the amount of money that could buy about five regular brands of phones to buy just one iPhone? I guess you know the answer. The reason is "quality" and that quality was a product of how much time he invested into developing the knowledge of the iPhone and producing the iPhone itself. Because he invested more time than other phone producers, he has become a lord in that territory with almost no rival. That is what happens when you invest more time into something than others. You become the best among equals. You become outstanding. If you can decide to invest all your time into giving birth to a quality product, the whole world will celebrate you and everyone will be in need of your product. The world cannot do without his products even though he is dead. He was able to leave his footprint in the sand of history but only because he understood the power of time conversion. He became great because he converted his time into quality products.

Mark Zuckerberg decided to be the lord over social networking and invested his time into developing a product; Facebook. A product that almost everyone in the world is enjoying. There is hardly a person in the world who is not on Facebook or who hasn't heard of Facebook. Mark Zuckerberg is only 32years old and has already ranked 5th richest man in the world with a net worth of $55.3b as at October 2016. He launched his product, Facebook on February 4, 2004, from his Harvard dormitory room at the age of 20yrs.

Now the question is how such a young man could be that wealthy and be the lord of social networking? The answer is "Time conversion" He invested his time into developing a product for the world. He converted his time into a product to benefit the world. Do you have any product for the world? Are you ready to convert your time into producing something that the world will remember you for? If your answer is no, then you may want to begin now to convert your time into products. Choose the territory you want to conquer and invest your time into developing yourself in that area until you become the best.

If you must record some greatness in your account before you leave this earth, you must value time and understand the importance of time conversion. Only through the conversion of time can greatness be bought. Only through the conversion of time can territories be conquered.

Your Territory of Choice Is Irrelevant, Time Conversion Is What Matters.

Someone may say, what if I am not a software developer or a computer literate? What if I am not into the world of science and technology? Well! The truth is that your territory doesn't have to be the same as that of the great men mentioned above. You may not even need to have a formal education to conquer your own territory. You necessarily do not have to have gone to the university to become great. Just decide your own territory. It could be in tailoring. It could be in music or dancing. It could be in the artistic painting. It could even be in carpentry. Whatever your territory is, doesn't matter. What matters is the amount of time you are ready to invest into it to become the king of that territory.

Let me further prove what I have been saying to you. Let's consider the story of Alex and Andrew who are both tailors and fashion designers. Alex always works on himself to improve his tailoring skills. He invests so much of his time about five hours every day besides normal working hours, learning and perfecting the act of tailoring. He invests his time every day doing self-development by converting his time into added value to himself. He invests his time into learning the latest technology in tailoring and researching what is in vogue in the fashion world. Alex turns his time into added value and doesn't allow his time to vanish into vanity. He blocks his time from just flying away by converting it into some form of products.

But Andrew just goes to work casually every day. He doesn't bother to add value to himself. He just goes to work like any regular tailor. He doesn't understand the principle of time conversion.

Andrew makes one suit in a month but Alex because of his proficiency makes twelve suits every month. At the end of the year, Andrew has learnt to make only twelve suits of average quality while Alex because of his added value and knowledge would have made one hundred and forty four suits of the best quality. What is the difference? The same time, one year given to both tailors but one person produced twelve products of low quality while the other produced one hundred and forty four products of highest quality. Equal time, different products. The difference is just that Alex invested his time into conquering his territory while Andrew wasted or probably just spent his time without converting it into added value.

If a company is in need of hundred quality suits for its workers every year, who do you think they will contact? Alex of course! If the president and ministers are to have a congress meeting and need to purchase quality suits in bulk, who do you think they will contact? Alex of course! If a guy is getting married at the end of the month and needs twelve suits for his groom's men at the end of the month, who do you think can do the job and meet up with the deadline? Alex of course!

You see, Alex has conquered his territory because he invested more time building himself. He has become lord over that area of calling. Andrew can't even compete with him in terms of products and wealth. Even if they both fix the same price for their suits, Alex will still be wealthier than Andrew because when Andrew is selling one suit a month Alex will be selling twelve suits that same month. Now Alex is making far more money than Andrew thanks to his time conversion. Remember again "money is made out of time" Now Alex has become a great and wealthy tailor because of the power of time conversion while Andrew is only an average tailor struggling to make ends meet. So it doesn't really matter your area of calling or the territory you have chosen. If you can invest quality time into it, you will definitely become the best and that will buy you greatness. You can be great in any area of life. Just learn to convert time into added value and tangible products. Stop wasting time, start investing time for that is the only way to greatness.

Dear friends, I believe now you have seen how money can be made out of time conversion. If you are financially poor it is because you have not converted your time into any product. Bill Gates converted time to Money, Warren Buffet did the same. The young Mark Zuckerberg did the same, you too can become wealthy but only thanks to the amount of time you are willing to convert into products.

If you have made up your mind to rank among the great and the rich of society, then it is time to put off every distraction and run away for your life. Let's proceed to the next chapter as I show you how to do that.

TIME PRINCIPLES
FROM CHAPTER NINE

1. Every human being is equally wealthy according to God's divine Providence.

2. We are all endowed with the wealth of time equally. Everybody that is born on the surface of this earth, has this wealth.

3. Solitude is a law that works for you no matter what. The law of conversion of time will work for you anytime. Whether you are a believer or not, solitude will give you the same result.

4. Money is a by-product of time. Money is the time that is well converted. Therefore time is the raw material from which money is made.

5. In life, everyone must decide in what area of life he or she wants to be great. You must choose what territory you want to conquer.

6. To become the king of that territory you must not allow any of your time pass without converting it into building your skills in that area of life.

7. You must, first of all, evolve the consciousness of being the best in whatever territory you choose to explore and then invest all your time into it and you will be amazed how easy it is to become great.

8. Therefore the way to becoming the best in your area of calling is to invest more time than anyone else in

that area of life. So you must decide what territory you want to conquer and give it all of your time.

9. The amount of time you invest into your products determines the quality of the products.

10. If you can decide to invest all your time into giving birth to a quality product, the whole world will celebrate you and everyone will be in need of your product.

HOW TO BECOME GREAT
THROUGH TIME CONVERSION

1. After deciding the territory you want to rule over, the next thing you must do is to invest your time into developing yourself and becoming the best in that territory.

2. You must arrest every passing time and convert it into growing your knowledge and prowess in that chosen field of influence.

3. If you don't want to just live an ordinary life, then you will have to be intentional about converting all your time into that which you have been called to do.

4. If you allow someone else to convert more time than you in your chosen territory, you automatically become a servant or a second class citizen in that territory and whoever it is who converted more time than you in that territory becomes your king and will lord it over you in that territory.

5. If you must record some greatness in your account before you leave this earth, you must value time and understand the importance of time conversion.

6. It doesn't really matter your area of calling or the territory you have chosen. If you can invest quality time into it, you will definitely become the best and that will buy you greatness.

7. It doesn't matter what your calling is, if you can invest all your time into it then greatness will become your reward.

8. Time is the raw material from which products are made and when products are sold, money is made.

9. Only when that time is converted can you produce something from it. You can only make wealth from a time well converted.

10. Only through the conversion of time can greatness be bought. Only through the conversion of time can territories be conquered.

CHAPTER 10

RUN FOR YOUR LIFE!

Wow! I am delighted to welcome you to the last chapter of this book. We have stated in this book that everybody including you has the potential to become great. I believe by now you have learnt so much on how you could buy greatness with your time. We have said in this book that the best thing you should do with your time in order to become great is to invest your time instead of wasting or just spending it. To invest your time is to convert it into some products that could benefit humanity. I have explained also how that your time is your life and if you allow your time melt away, your life melts alongside with it. To prevent your time from just melting into vanity you must race against time and stand in the way of time so you could convert it to tangible products.

However, the best way to arrest time is to convert it into a treasure called solitude. You have learnt that solitude is the greatest treasure and through it, you can rebuild your life, reorder your life and solve life's problems. To become the best in any area of life, you must learn to practise the rule of ten thousand hours because only through it can you gain mastery. The desire of most people on earth is to make money and money seems to be the greatest motivation in life for a lot of people. However, to become financially buoyant and rank among the richest men in the world, you must learn to convert time into money. This is because money is made out of time.

Having learnt all these principles, the only thing that could prevent you from becoming great are the distractions that you are faced with every day of your life. If you truly want to apply the lessons that you've learnt from this book, then you must run from every distraction. It is for this reason that I invite you to read this last chapter so as to be able to run for your life.

THE DISTRACTIONS OF OUR GENERATION

"I felt like I wasn't living thoroughly enough — I was distracted in ways I wouldn't be if I'd been born in 1929."
MIRANDA JULY

One tragic thing I have observed in this generation is that there are too many distractions. Almost everyone has got a distraction or two with the social media being perhaps the greatest distraction for the majority. Technology has its huge advantages but also has its negative effects. The digital age has got enough games and Apps to distract the interested population. In the past, people could walk away from their distractions to go find a quiet place to go invest their time focusing on a particular task like reading, writing, meditation etc. But the ugly side of the digital age is that we carry our distractions with us wherever we go. It is either you are chatting with someone on Facebook, or you are checking pictures on Instagram. If you are not snap-chatting then you could be chatting on WhatsApp. Again, you could either be playing Candy crush and Criminal case or pirates and Soccer game. All of these distractions eat up your time unknowingly to you. While you are busy engaging in anyone of the above mentioned distractions, your life is gradually disappearing. Your time is diminishing per every second and minute that passes. Your time keeps flying away into vanity while you dine with your distractions. Your life keeps diminishing while you waste your time feeding your distractions. The reason why this generation is greatly distracted is because people do not know the value of time. This generation does not understand the wealth of time. No wonder there are only a few superstars and great men emerging from this generation. Most surprisingly is the fact that people do not know what to do with time. This ignorance of what to do with time is the number one reason why people get bored so easily when alone with nothing to do. Technology, therefore, has found a way to rescue the ignorant multitude from boredom by presenting this generation with as many digital gadgets, apps, and games that could solve the boredom problem. However, technology does not announce to you that these gadgets will steal your time and your life from you gradually. You are not told that while you try to eliminate your boredom by playing games and chatting on social media or watching movies and making unnecessary phone calls; your life is diminishing into vanity.

At this stage of my life, I don't even carry my phone because people just call you from nowhere and for no reason just wanting to say hi and to chat with you. You see, the ability to get rid of your phone is an advantage that will help you overcome distractions. You also need the ability to overcome other distractions like television. Thank God over twenty years ago, I have gotten rid of television and it's not a big distraction to me anymore. I learnt how to switch off all distractions and that gave me the ability to not waste my time on frivolities. You too must develop such abilities because I know so much pressure is on all of us to waste time and to just trivialize it. There is so much pressure on us to try to overcome boredom by spending time on frivolities.

People who understand how to convert their time into useful products do not complain of boredom. They have too many important tasks to accomplish that they can hardly get bored. They understand that those distractions are a waste of time and life. Such people who do not waste their life truly understand the importance of time.

So when you understand the value of time, the resource and the wealth of time, you will be running away from the crowd, you will begin to run away from distractions. If you understand that a wasted time is a wasted life, you will start running away from television, you will begin to run away from movies, you will run away from games like criminal case and candy crush. Once you understand the wealth of time, you will begin to run for your life. You will run away from anything that looks like a distraction. Things that use to interest you before will become detestable to you. When you understand that through the power of conversion in solitude you can become great, so many things you've been wasting your time on will no longer interest you. You will even run away from some friends. You will need to run away from champions' league and premier league. You are running for your life because you now know that you need to convert that time. That you need to convert every minute and second of your life. You have come to understand that your life is diminishing rapidly if you don't convert it into valuable products.

SCHOOL, JOB, AND PURPOSE

Another distraction that deviates people from their God given purpose and calling is the distraction of job and formal education. You need to be careful. Everybody is in a hurry to go to school just so that they could get a job after they graduate. The focus is no longer on fulfilling purpose but on going to school and getting a job afterwards. Society has so deceived us that people no longer care if there is any such thing as purpose and divine calling. So a man spends his entire life just pursuing school and job with no interest in finding out about why he was created in the first place. How tragic it is to find that an entire lifetime is wasted in pursuit of distractions while purpose is neglected. Do not neglect your purpose.

If you really understand the treasure and the wealth of time, you will be rejoicing that they have fired you from your job. You will be rejoicing that the class room school system is no longer holding your time captive. Instead of you pouring out your life and giving out your life and exchanging it for a porridge called salary, instead of selling out your life bit by bit until you are old and empty and until you become so old that they send you off to die in retirement, you should come to realisation that you could actually multiply and reproduce your life through the power of time conversion.

If I were you, I would multiply my life by converting it into something tangible. I would run away from distractions. Please run away for your life now to convert it into a product that worth more than your peanut salary. Go and convert your time into the treasure called solitude. Don't trivialize the fact that your life is diminishing. Run for your life. Save your life and convert it to something worth more than salary.

Instead of exchanging your life for some coins and some pennies, you could actually take charge of your life. You can run away to take control of your time. When you run for your life, you will become the one deciding how you use your time. You will be the one deciding that you are not going to pour out your life anymore. You will no longer allow the school system or the work system to decide what you do with your time. When you run for your life, you become the boss of your life and you can convert your life into any product of your choice. When you run for your life, you are going to start, conserving it, you will begin investing it and multiplying it and converting it. You will start reproducing and duplicating your life and you are going to populate the earth with your products. You are going to saturate the earth with your seeds. Therefore to run for your life, you must first identify your distractions and make up your mind never to allow your distractions determine what you do with your time. The next step is to switch off your distractions and run, quit your distractions and run. Run! Run for your life!

STEVE JOBS RAN FOR HIS LIFE

I am sure you have heard of the name **Steve Jobs.** If you probably are using an iPad or an iPhone then Steve jobs live with you every day. Steve job is dead but he lives with you every day through his product, through his seed. However, there will be no iPhone or iPad if Steve jobs didn't run for his life. He could not have given birth to his products if he didn't run for his life.

The Mac, the iPod, heck, even Buzz Lightyear probably wouldn't have existed had Steve Jobs stayed in school. He dropped out of Reed College after just six months. He would go on to eventually found Apple, NeXT Computer, and Pixar. If he didn't come out of the formal school system, he would have probably spent his time learning just what society has scheduled for him to learn. He would not have had the time to research on his personal dreams and area of calling. He would probably just graduate and become a working slave spending his time to enriching his boss. But thanks to his dropping out of the formal school system, he was able to invest time into his calling and personal aspirations so much so that he became the innovator, visionary and Genius whose achievements the whole world is talking about and celebrating today.

Do you know that there are millions of people who are just spending their time in one college or university studying courses that they were never born to study? The majority of the students in our universities all around the world are studying courses which they should have no business with at all. There are people with awesome talents and unique callings that do not need the formal education system to help them fulfil their callings but are however just following the crowd to attend those universities. Some waste four five or six years of their lives studying what they know they have no passion nor the intellectual strength for. If the time spent going to a formal school was invested into developing their talents and area of calling, they would have become one of the best innovators, actors, painters, athletes, musicians or dancers in the world.

The best thing you should do to your self is to find out what unique talents and callings you have been endowed with and invest the rest of your life into developing and building yourself up so that you could be the best in that area of life. Do not be distracted by the formal school system. I know it may surprise you to hear me call the formal school system a distraction. Yes, it is a distraction for the multitude of people who's calling and talents are not linked to it. It is a distraction from the fulfilment of purpose. It is a distraction from the fulfilment of destiny. The formal school system has prevented many from becoming their best selves. The reason is because the time they would have used to build themselves up for the fulfilment of their purpose was ignorantly dedicated to a school curriculum which had nothing to do with their purpose and unique destinies. They allow themselves to be enslaved by a school curriculum which does not favour their purpose or life's calling.

Our streets are littered with university graduates holding paper certificates and looking for a way to enslave themselves again under a boss in the name of looking for a job. Our offices are filled with people working their lives out to enrich their boss, government or company. They all have been distracted from their original God given purposes and are now settling for the lesser life of a salary earner. My intention here is to draw your attention to the fact that the greatest innovators and history makers of our world were not great because of the formal school system but because of self- development through the proper investment and conversion of time. Like I said before if you really understand the treasure and the wealth of time, you will be rejoicing that the class room school system is not holding your time captive. You will be rejoicing that they have fired you from your work.

For Steve Jobs, he understood that to truly do great work and impact the world with it, one must run for his life and set himself apart to do that which he was born to do. To truly be satisfied in life, you must invest your time into doing what you were born to do instead of wasting your time trying to impress a boss or a company doing a job that you were not born for. Therefore your first priority should be to find out what work you were born to do and then secondly invest your time into doing it and you will be named among the great minds and geniuses in your generation in the nearest future.

"The only way to be truly satisfied is to do what you believe is great work, and the only way to do great work is to love what you do. If you haven't found it yet, keep looking, and don't settle. As with all matters of the heart, you'll know when you find it. And like any great relationship, it just gets better and better as the years roll on. So keep looking, don't settle."
STEVE JOBS

It is only when you run away from what society wants you to do with your time and then invest that time into doing what you were born to do; that you can attain greatness and live a fulfilled life. Millions of people today are spending their time doing what society wants them to do, not investing it into doing what they were born to do. If you wake up early every morning running to work to do some jobs for your boss or your government and get paid for it by the end of the month, you are simply spending your whole time doing what society has imposed on you to do not what you were born to do. To truly invest your time into doing what you were born to do, you should be running away from jobs not running to jobs. The only way to saturate the earth with your products like Steve Jobs is to invest your time doing what you were born to do. For you, it may be that you need to quit the formal school system and start self-education in your area of calling. You may also need to quit your job and start investing your time into working for yourself and producing products in your area of calling. I am going to leave you with this speech by Steve Jobs.

> *"I'm pretty sure none of this would have happened if I hadn't been fired from Apple,"* he said at Stanford in 2005. *"It was awful-tasting medicine, but I guess the patient needed it. Sometimes life hits you in the head with a brick."*
>
> STEVE JOBS

After he resigned from Apple, he went on to invest his time into working for himself and saturating the earth with his products. In About ten years later Steve Jobs has filled the earth with one product or another including the iTunes (2003), the MacBook (2006), the iPhone (2007) and the iPad (2010). All these were possible only thanks to the fact that he ran for his life and began to invest his time into his destiny and area of calling. If you, therefore, must be numbered among the great, you too must run for your life.

You must run from any distraction. You must run from any slavery of job. You must run from any slavery of a formal school system's curriculum. You must run from low yielding activities and frivolities of life. You must run from time wasters and life wasters. You will only need to run towards your destiny and area of calling. You will only need to run towards solitude and time conversion. You will only need to run towards self-education. You will only need to run towards the development of your talents, crafts, and gifting. I charge you to run. Run! Go perfect your crafts. Run! Go use your creativity. Run! Go create your products. Run! Go rule your world. Run! Run for your life!

> *"When you're socially awkward, you're isolated more than usual, and when you're isolated more than usual, your creativity is less compromised by what has already been said and done. All your hope in life starts to depend on your craft, so you try to perfect it. One reason I stay isolated more than the average person is to keep my creativity as fierce as possible. Being the odd one out may have its temporary disadvantages, but more importantly, it has its permanent advantages."*
>
> CRISS JAMI, KILLOSOPHY

TIME PRINCIPLES
FROM CHAPTER TEN

1. Your time keeps flying away into vanity
    while you dine with your distractions. Your
    life keeps diminishing while you waste
    your time feeding your distractions.

2. This generation does not understand the wealth of
    time. No wonder there are only a few superstars
    and great men emerging from this generation.

3. This ignorance of what to do with time is the
    number one reason why people get bored so
    easily when alone with nothing to do.

4. You are not told that while you try to eliminate your
    boredom by playing games and chatting on social
    media or watching movies and making unnecessary
    phone calls; your life is diminishing into vanity.

5. I know so much pressure is on all of us to
    waste time and to just trivialize it. There is
    so much pressure on us to try to overcome
    boredom by spending time on frivolities.

6. People who understand how to convert their
    time into useful products do not complain of
    boredom. They have too many important tasks
    to accomplish that they can hardly get bored.

7. Such people who do not waste their life truly
    understand the importance of time.

8. When you understand the value of time, the resource and the wealth of time, you will be running away from the crowd.

9. Once you understand the wealth of time, you will begin to run for your life. You will run away from anything that looks like a distraction.

10. When you understand that through the power of conversion in solitude you can become great, so many things you've been wasting your time on will no longer interest you. You will even run away from some friends.

HOW TO BECOME GREAT
THROUGH TIME CONVERSION

1. You see, the ability to get rid of your phone is an advantage that will help you overcome distractions. You also need the ability to overcome other distractions like television.

2. You will even run away from some friends. You will need to run away from champions' league and premier league. You are running for your life because you now know that you need to convert that time.

3. How tragic it is to find that an entire lifetime is wasted in pursuit of distractions while purpose is neglected. Do not neglect your purpose.

4. Another distraction that deviates people from their God given purpose and calling is the distraction of job and formal education. You need to be careful.

5. Instead of you pouring out your life and giving out your life and exchanging it for a porridge called salary, instead of selling out your life bit by bit until you are old and empty and until you become so old that they send you off to die in retirement, you should come to the realisation that you could actually multiply and reproduce your life through the power of time conversion.

6. Instead of exchanging your life for some coins and some pennies, you could actually take

charge of your life right now. You can run
away to take control of your time right now.

7. When you run for your life, you will become
the one deciding how you use your time. You
will be the one deciding that you are not going
to pour out your life anymore. You will no
longer allow the school system or the work
system to decide what you do with your time.

8. When you run for your life, you become the boss
of your life and you can convert your life into any
product of your choice. When you run for your life,
you are going to start, conserving it, you will begin
investing it and multiplying it and converting it.

9. You will start reproducing and duplicating
your life and you are going to populate the
earth with your products. You are going
to saturate the earth with your seeds.

10. To run for your life, you must first identify
your distractions and make up your
mind never to allow your distractions
determine what you do with your time.

CONCLUSION

Dear friends, I do hope you will apply the principles and truth revealed in this book. It is my utmost desire to see you live the great life that you were born to live. I believe you can become great because the wealth of time needed to achieve greatness is in your possession. I believe now that you understand the value of time and the principles of time conversion that you will begin to give an account of every second and minute of your life that passes. I believe you will begin to invest and convert every passing time into some products. My prayer for you is that you no longer trivialize time and that you value it so much so that you will always invest it. I look forward to seeing you at the top. Go! Invest your time! Go! Convert your time into products for the world is waiting for your products!

Go! Buy greatness with your time! Go!
Greatness is in you!
For The Love Of God, Church And Nation.
Dr. Sunday Adelaja

SUNDAY ADELAJA'S
BIOGRAPHY

Pastor Sunday Adelaja is the Founder and Senior Pastor of The Embassy of the Blessed Kingdom of God for All Nations Church in Kyiv, Ukraine.

Sunday Adelaja is a Nigerian-born Leader, Thinker, Philosopher, Transformation Strategist, Pastor, Author and Innovator who lives in Kiev, Ukraine.

At 19, he won a scholarship to study in the former Soviet Union. He completed his master's program in Belorussia State University with distinction in journalism.

At 33, he had built the largest evangelical church in Europe — The Embassy of the Blessed Kingdom of God for All Nations.

Sunday Adelaja is one of the few individuals in our world who has been privileged to speak in the United Nations, Israeli Parliament, Japanese Parliament and the United States Senate.

The movement he pioneered has been instrumental in reshaping lives of people in the Ukraine, Russia and about 50 other nations where he has his branches.

His congregation, which consists of ninety-nine percent white Europeans, is a cross-cultural model of the church for the 21st century.

His life mission is to advance the Kingdom of God on earth by

raising a generation of history makers who will live for a cause larger, bigger and greater than themselves. Those who will live like Jesus and transform every sphere of the society in every nation as a model of the Kingdom of God on earth.

His economic empowerment program has succeeded in raising over 200 millionaires in the short period of three years.

Sunday Adelaja is the author of over 300 books, many of which are translated into several languages including Russian, English, French, Chinese, German, etc.

His work has been widely reported by world media outlets such as The Washington Post, The Wall Street Journal, New York Times, Forbes, Associated Press, Reuters, CNN, BBC, German, Dutch and French national television stations.

Pastor Sunday is happily married to his "Princess" Bose Dere-Adelaja. They are blessed with three children: Perez, Zoe and Pearl.

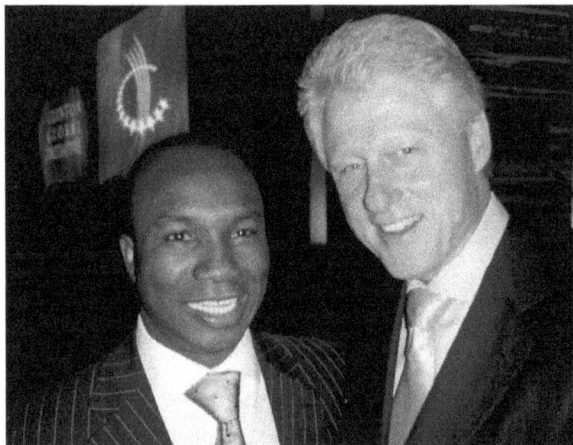

Bill Clinton — 42Nd President Of The United States (1993–2001), Former Arcansas State Governor

Ariel "Arik" Sharon — Israeli Politician, Israeli Prime Minister (2001–2006)

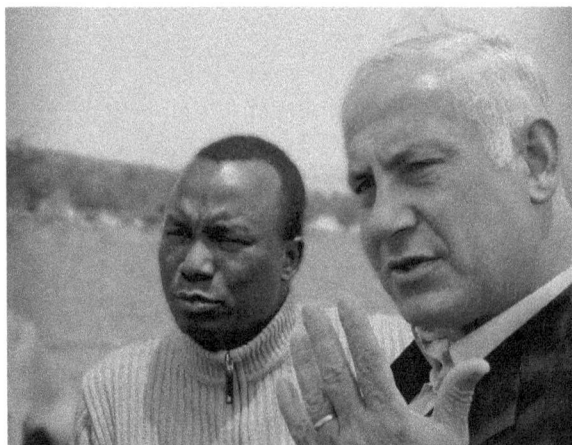

Benjamin Netanyahu — Statesman Of Israel. Israeli Prime Minister (1996–1999), Acting Prime Minister (From 2009)

Jean ChrEtien —
Canadian Politician,
20Th Prime Minister Of
Canada, Minister Of Justice
Of Canada, Head Of Liberan
Party Of Canada

Rudolph Giuliani —
American Political Actor,
Mayor Of New York Served
From 1994 To 2001. Actor
Of Republican Party

Colin Powell —
Is An American Statesman
And A Retired Four-Star
General In The Us Army,
65Th United States Secretary
Of State

Peter J. Daniels —
Is A Well-Known And
Respected Australian
Christian International
Business Statesman Of
Substance

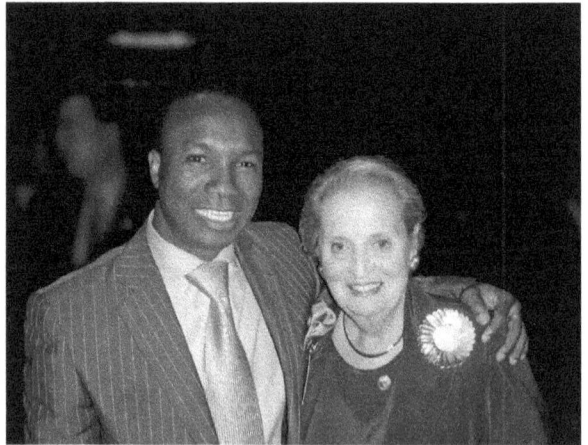

Madeleine
Korbel Albright —
An American Politician And
Diplomat, 64Th United States
Secretary Of State

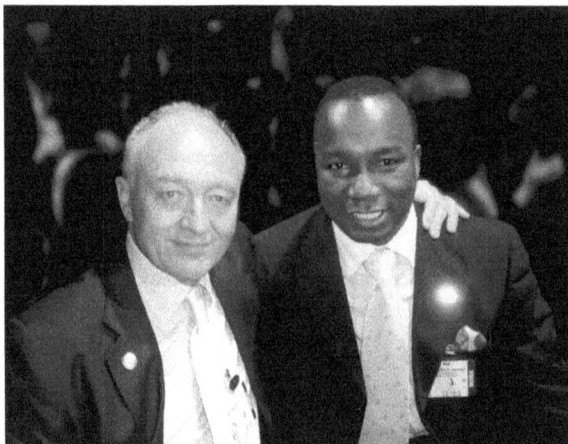

Kenneth Robert
Livingstone —
An English Politician,
1St Mayor Of London
(4 May 2000 – 4 May
2008), Labour Party
Representative

Sir Richard Charles Nicholas Branson — English Business Magnate, Investor And Philanthropist. He Founded The *Virgin Group,* Which Controls More Than 400 Companies

Mel Gibson — American Actor And Filmmaker

Chuck Norris — American Martial Artist, Actor, Film Producer And Screenwriter

Christopher Tucker —
American Actor
And Comedian

Bernice Albertine King —
American Minister Best
Known As The Youngest
Child Of Civil Rights Leaders
Martin Luther King Jr. And
Coretta Scott King Andrew

Andrew Young — American
Politician, Diplomat, And
Activist, 14Th United States
Ambassador To The United
Nations, 55Th Mayor Of
Atlanta

General Wesley Kanne Clark — 4-Star General And Nato Supreme Allied Commander

Dr. Sunday Adelaja's family: Perez, Pearl, Zoe and Pastor Bose Adelaja

FOLLOW
SUNDAY ADELAJA
ON SOCIAL MEDIA

Subscribe And Read Pastor Sunday's Blog:

www.sundayadelajablog.com

Follow these links and listen to over 200

of Pastor Sunday`s Messages free of charge:

http://sundayadelajablog.com/content/

Follow Pastor Sunday on Twitter:

www.twitter.com/official_pastor

Join Pastor Sunday's Facebook page to stay in touch:

www.facebook.com/pastor.

sunday.adelaja

Visit our websites for more

information about Pastor

Sunday's ministry:

http://www.godembassy.com

http://www.pastorsunday.com

http://sundayadelaja.de

CONTACT

FOR DISTRIBUTION OR TO ORDER
BULK COPIES OF THIS BOOK,
PLEASE CONTACT US:

USA

CORNERSTONE PUBLISHING

info@thecornerstonepublishers.com

+1 (516) 547-4999

www.thecornerstonepublishers.com

AFRICA

SUNDAY ADELAJA MEDIA LTD.

E-mail: btawolana@hotmail.com

+2348187518530, +2348097721451, +2348034093699

LONDON, UK

PASTOR ABRAHAM GREAT

abrahamagreat@gmail.com

+447711399828, +441908538141

KIEV, UKRAINE

pa@godembassy.org

Mobile: +380674401958

MONEY WON'T make you Rich
GOD'S PRINCIPLES FOR TRUE WEALTH, PROSPERITY AND SUCCESS
SUNDAY ADELAJA

"IF NIGERIA DOES NOT SUCCEED, WHO ELSE CAN SUCCEED?"
- Peter Eigen, Transparency International (Germany)
NIGERIA AND THE LEADERSHIP QUESTION
PROFFERING SOLUTIONS TO NIGERIA'S LEADERSHIP PROBLEM
SUNDAY ADELAJA
BEST SELLING AUTHOR OF CHURCHSHIFT

MYLES MUNROE
... FINDING ANSWERS TO WHY GOOD PEOPLE DIE TRAGIC AND EARLY DEATHS
SUNDAY ADELAJA

THE KINGDOM DRIVEN LIFE
Thy Kingdom Come, Thy will be Done on Earth . . .
SUNDAY ADELAJA
BEST SELLING AUTHOR OF CHURCHSHIFT

CHURCH SHIFT
SUNDAY ADELAJA

WHO AM I?
WHY AM I HERE?
SUNDAY ADELAJA
BEST SELLING AUTHOR OF CHURCHSHIFT

ONLY GOD can save NIGERIA: What a Myth!
SUNDAY ADELAJA
The Author of Nigeria and his Leadership Question

MONEY IS A GOOD SLAVE, BUT A BAD MASTER
STOP
WORKING FOR UNCLE SAM
SUNDAY ADELAJA

The MOUNTAIN of IGNORANCE
The Greatest Problem of Man is Not Sin or Satan, it is Ignorance
#1 BEST SELLER
SUNDAY ADELAJA

OLORUNWA
Лороги Жизни

INSULTED by UNGODLINESS
RAISING A GENERATION OF THE PROVOKED IN EVERY NATION
SUNDAY ADELAJA
BEST SELLING AUTHOR OF CHURCHSHIFT

#1 BESTSELLING AUTHOR
HOW TO REGAIN YOUR LOST YEARS
SUNDAY ADELAJA

BEST SELLING BOOKS BY DR. SUNDAY ADELAJA
AVAILABLE ON AMAZON.COM AND OKADABOOKS.COM

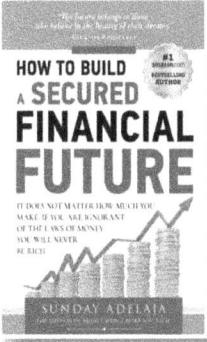

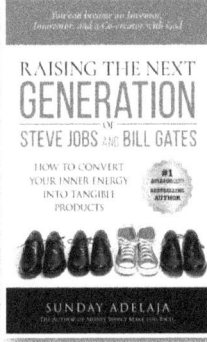

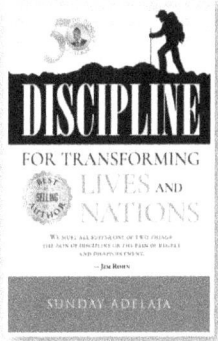

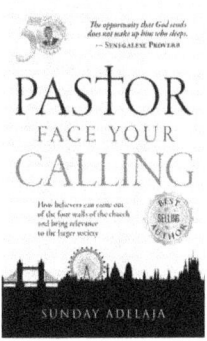

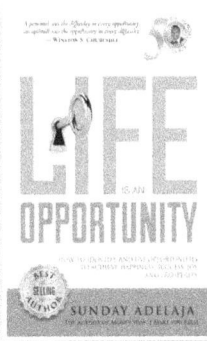

HOW TO BUILD A SECURED FINANCIAL FUTURE — SUNDAY ADELAJA

CREATE YOUR OWN NET WORTH — SUNDAY ADELAJA

RAISING THE NEXT GENERATION OF STEVE JOBS AND BILL GATES — SUNDAY ADELAJA

POVERTY MINDSET VS ABUNDANCE MINDSET — SUNDAY ADELAJA

WHY YOU MUST URGENTLY BECOME A WORKAHOLIC — SUNDAY ADELAJA

HOW TO BECOME GREAT THROUGH TIME CONVERSION — SUNDAY ADELAJA

The NIGERIAN ECONOMY THE WAY FORWARD — SUNDAY ADELAJA

DISCIPLINE FOR TRANSFORMING LIVES AND NATIONS — SUNDAY ADELAJA

PASTOR FACE YOUR CALLING — SUNDAY ADELAJA

WHERE THERE IS PROBLEM THERE IS MONEY — SUNDAY ADELAJA

LIFE IS AN OPPORTUNITY — SUNDAY ADELAJA

The CREATIVE and INNOVATIVE POWER of a GENIUS — SUNDAY ADELAJA

GOLDEN JUBILEE SERIES BOOKS
BY DR. SUNDAY ADELAJA

FOR DISTRIBUTION OR TO ORDER BULK COPIES OF THIS BOOKS, PLEASE CONTACT US:

USA | CORNERSTONE PUBLISHING
E-mail: info@thecornerstonepublishers.com, +1 (516) 547-4999
www.thecornerstonepublishers.com

AFRICA | SUNDAY ADELAJA MEDIA LTD.
E-mail: btawolana@hotmail.com
+2348187518530, +2348097721451, +2348034093699

LONDON, UK | PASTOR ABRAHAM GREAT
E-mail: abrahamagreat@gmail.com, +447711399828, +441908538141

KIEV, UKRAINE |
E-mail: pa@godembassy.org, Mobile: +380674401958